BUILDING THE INFORMATION HIGHWAY

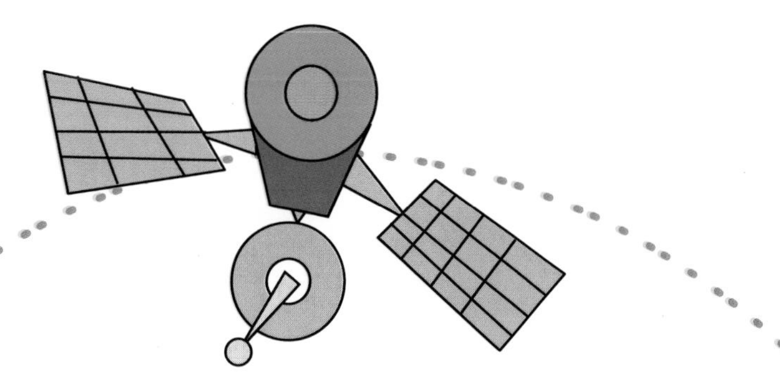

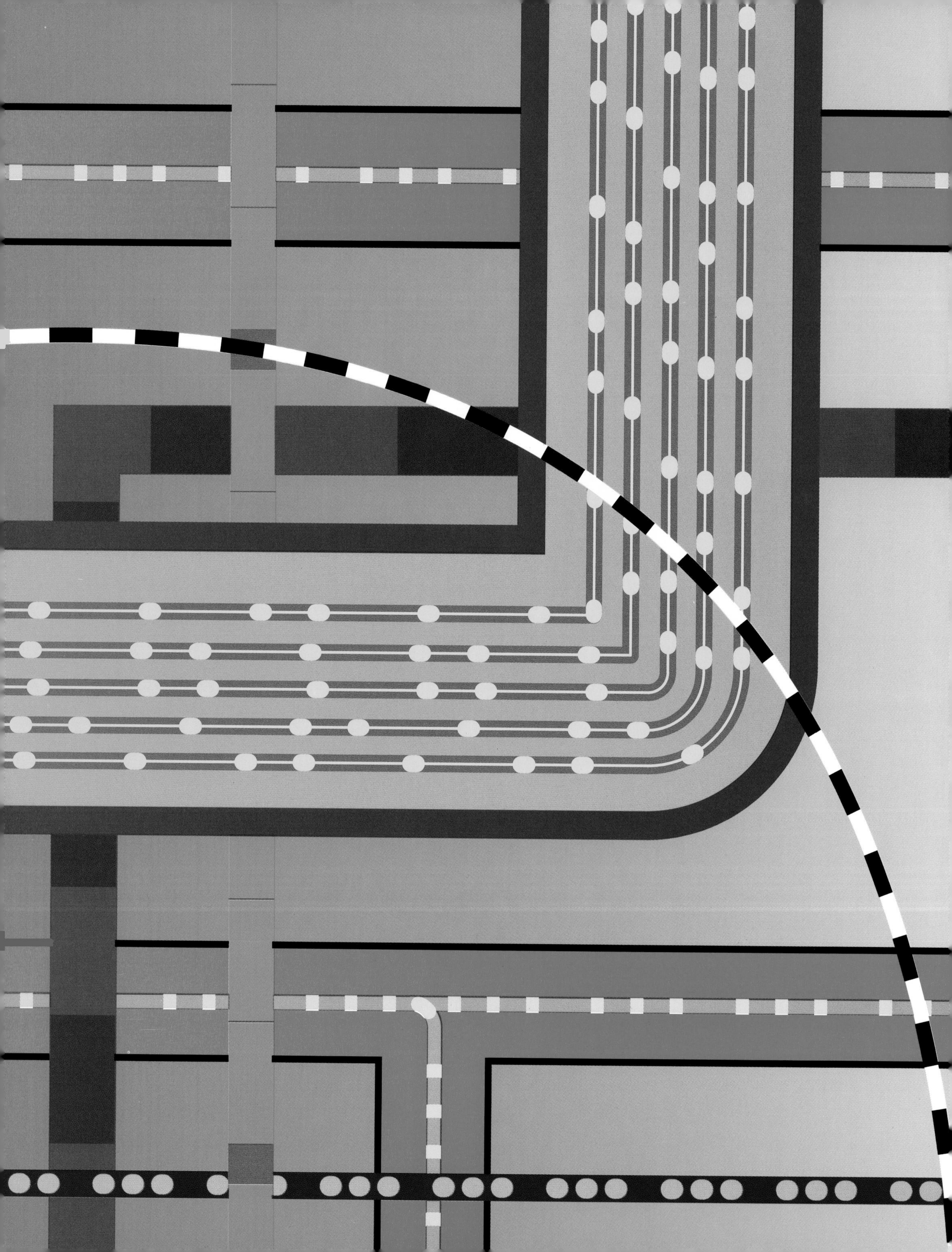

BUILDING THE INFORMATION HIGHWAY

LES FREED AND FRANK J. DERFLER, JR.

Illustrated by
CHAD KUBO

Ziff-Davis Press
Emeryville, California

Development Editor	Valerie Haynes Perry
Copy Editor	Jan Jue
Technical Reviewer	John Taschek
Project Coordinator	Cort Day
Proofreader	Carol Burbo
Cover Illustration	Regan Honda and Chad Kubo
Cover Design	Carrie English
Book Design	Carrie English
Principal Technical Illustrator	Chad Kubo
Additional Technical Illustrator	Nina Melinda Reimer
Word Processing	Howard Blechman
Page Layout	Bruce Lundquist
Indexer	Anne Leach

Ziff-Davis Press books are produced on a Macintosh computer system with the following applications: FrameMaker®, Microsoft® Word, QuarkXPress®, Adobe Illustrator®, Adobe Photoshop®, Adobe Streamline™, MacLink®*Plus*, Aldus® FreeHand™, Collage Plus™.

If you have comments or questions or would like to receive a free catalog, call or write:
Ziff-Davis Press
5903 Christie Avenue
Emeryville, CA 94608
1-800-688-0448

ISBN 1-56276-126-9

Manufactured in the United States of America

This book is printed on paper that contains 20% total recycled fibers of which 50% is de-inked postconsumer fiber.

10 9 8 7 6 5 4 3 2

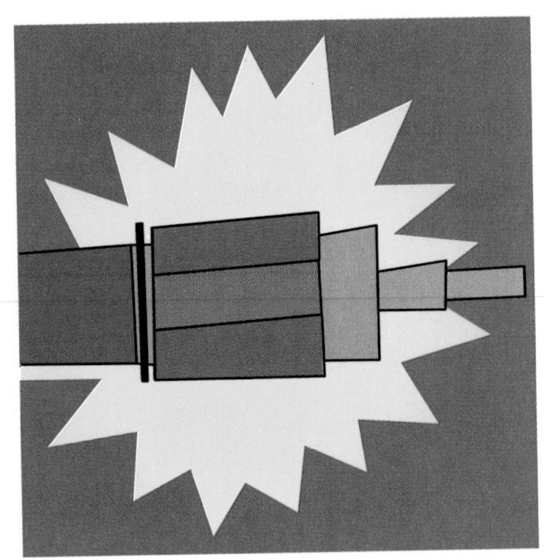

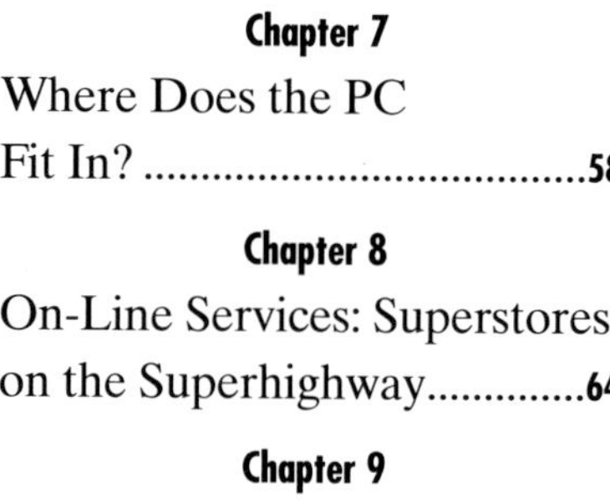

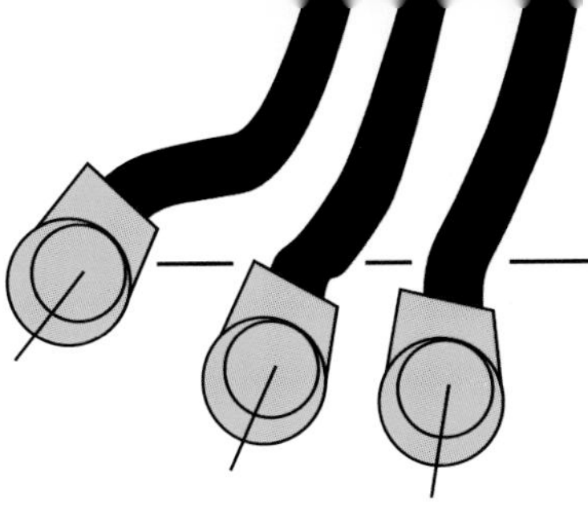

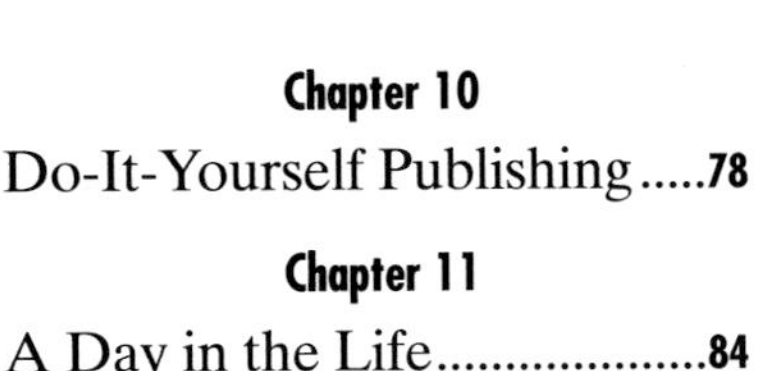

PART 3

Building a Digital World

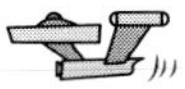

96

Will the data highway roll through your front door or will it pass you by? Why should you care? While we keep our feet firmly planted on solid ground, we're going to give you a helicopter view of the digital highway, which is how we will refer to the information highway. All along the way, we'll try to put things into perspective and to cut through the haze of hyperbole and special interests. We'll include enough history to show you the road behind, enough technology to show you the road ahead, and enough common sense to tell you what it all means.

Evolution, skepticism, and sky-high optimism have always been integral parts of our communications systems. When Alexander Graham Bell's original Bell Telephone Company began service in the late 1800s, most people dismissed the telephone as a technical curiosity with limited commercial value. There was nothing so important, the naysayers contended, that required immediate voice communication. One hundred years later, American Telephone and Telegraph (AT&T), the successor to Bell's original company, had become the largest company in the world, operating over 100 million telephones and employing over 1 million people worldwide. It's safe to say that those naysayers were dead wrong.

In the years since Bell's first commercial telephone, the world has witnessed the coming of radio, motion pictures, television, the computer, and hundreds of other important innovations. These communication tools have had a profound impact on all our lives. Since their beginnings, the technologies of motion pictures, television, and the telephone have evolved along parallel (but separate and often incompatible) tracks. The arrival of cheap computer power is now making it possible for those tracks to merge, thanks to a phenomenon called *convergence*.

Convergence is the marriage of television, telephone, and computer data communications into a single, integrated, compatible network. The result of this convergence is a new, worldwide digital network—the digital highway. As such, convergence represents the next milestone in the ongoing development of our communications technology.

Each industry or company has its own unique perspective on convergence. Companies with a television orientation see everything in terms of TV. The big companies in the cable TV business are developing products that will use your TV set as your interface to convergence. Companies coming into the convergence market from the computer side of the industry see things a bit differently. They see the digital highway as a huge pipeline that will allow computers to exchange vast amounts of information quickly and cheaply.

The history of the communications industry is one of constant change, and convergence is simply the latest in a long series of changes. In this book, we explain the technology behind the digital highway and the likely uses for that technology. We'll also take a look at our existing communications infrastructure so that you'll better understand the changes taking place and see how to make them work to your benefit.

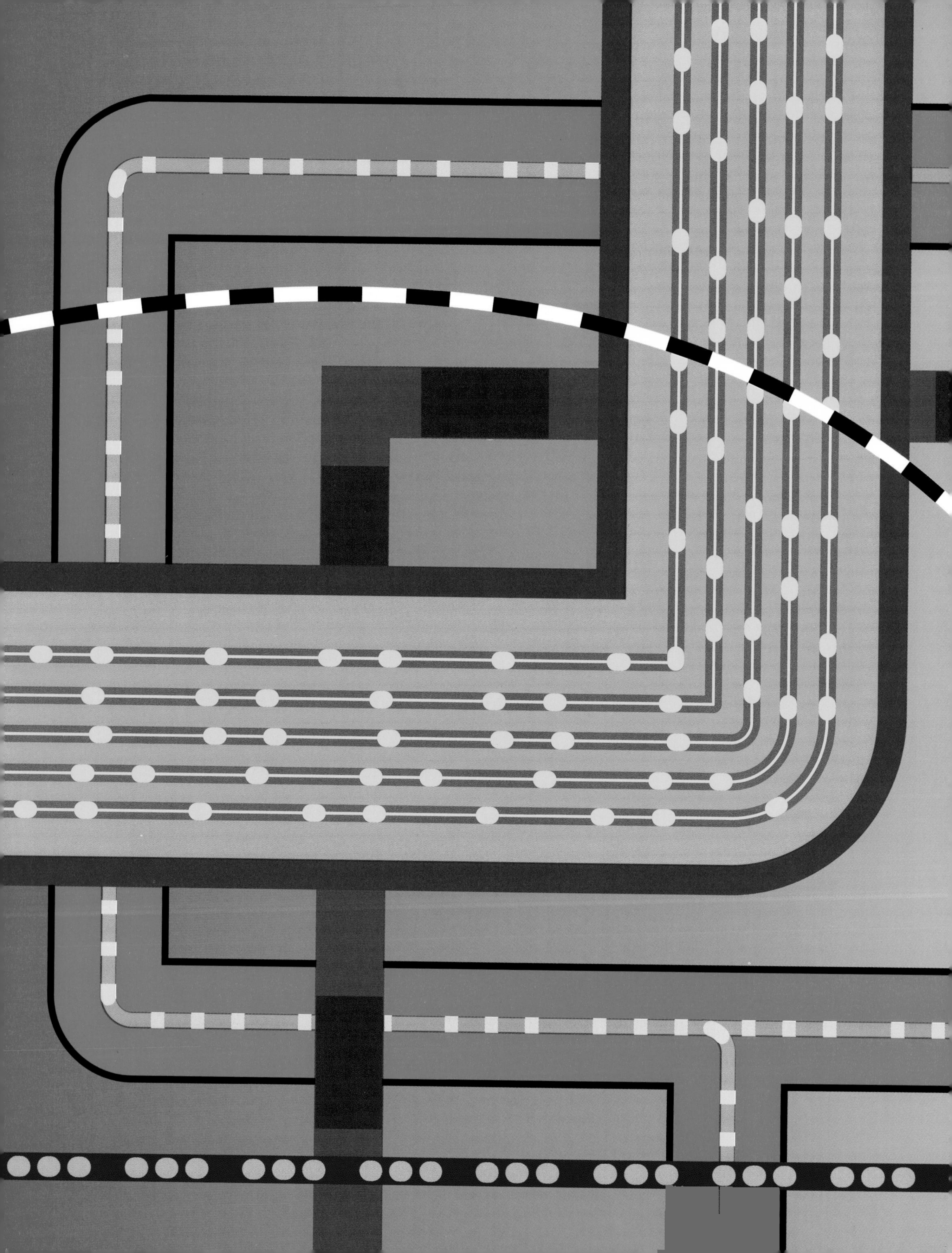

LEARNING TO DRIVE

ONE DAY some time ago, the term "information superhighway" slipped quietly into your daily life. Like most of us, you probably didn't invite this term in to visit—it just started appearing in your morning paper (on both the business page and in the comics), popping up now and then on CNN and "Nightly Business Report," and becoming the topic of dinner party discussion. Depending who you ask, the information superhighway encompasses everything from today's existing Internet network to 500-channel television to interactive, real-time virtual reality. Estimates of completion time range from "now" to "2010" and beyond. As usual, the truth probably lies somewhere in the middle.

In an industry infamous for premature product announcements, outrageous product claims, and the occasional outright lie, the media feeding frenzy surrounding the "digital highway" (the term we'll use throughout this book) has established new highs for hyperbole. Our goal in this book is not to throw more food into the media shark pool, but rather to provide a broad overview of what the digital highway can and may become.

To tell the truth, we don't really like the term digital highway, nor do we like to think of it entirely in the future tense. The highway metaphor is already overused, and it doesn't begin to explain the vast scope and breadth of the ongoing communications revolution. We say *ongoing* because this is a revolution that began over 15 years ago, when one of the first personal computers spoke its first binary words through one of the first PC modems. And as with most revolutions, this one will involve conflicts, skirmishes, and boardroom battles among several factions.

Like a barroom brawl, the edges of the communications battle zone have already expanded to include players who weren't even looking for or expecting a fight. Virtually every company involved in communications, entertainment, and information services is or will be involved. Huge companies like Sony, AT&T, GTE, MCI, the Regional Bell Operating Companies (RBOCs), major TV networks such as CBS, NBC, ABC, and many other, smaller companies will need to adapt to the new world of communications. Otherwise, they will be left behind by more nimble, forward-thinking competitors. New advances in technology and new alliances between providers and distributors of information will continue to challenge the old information and entertainment infrastructures.

In the United States, public interest in the digital highway took off during the 1992 presidential election when candidates Bill Clinton and Al Gore underlined the need for a "National Information Infrastructure" (NII). At that time, the Clinton campaign prepared a position paper that incorporated ideas presented by several computer industry leaders. Since taking office, Clinton and his administration have kept the NII a top priority and have issued a plan to get the NII ball rolling. A major part of this plan is to get private industry involved from the start, with the U.S. government providing seed money for trial projects. Other key points of the Clinton plan include: a promise to review and revise any government regulations that impede the operation of the NII network; creation of a "Universal Service Plan" that will ensure affordable access to all; and the establishment of standards to ensure information security and individual privacy, as well as the protection of intellectual property rights.

While the NII plan is part of an official government policy, it is not the only set of blueprints for the digital highway. The NII plan concerns itself primarily with increasing the public's access to government and educational resources. Several proposals for an all-digital, high-speed public data network have been around for years. One set of standards known as ISDN (Integrated Services Digital Network) is already widely used in Europe. As we will see, there are hundreds of players competing for a piece of the digital highway pie, and their plans far exceed the NII's goals.

Much of the underlying communications technology to be used as building material for the digital highway is not new. The basic idea behind the various proposed structures for the digital highway is to take one (or more) of these communications technologies and marry it to a wealth of services. Some of the services have present-day counterparts, but dozens of companies are lining up to create entirely new types of services. The underlying communications technologies range from our familiar analog telephone and cable television service at one extreme to high-speed, digital, fiber-optic cable connections at the other.

Major advances in computer and data communications technology have put the PC head-to-head with the television set as the world's entertainment vehicle of choice. A surprising number of people now spend more time in front of their PCs than their TVs, and several million people already subscribe to commercial on-line services like CompuServe, Prodigy, and America Online. Millions more use the Internet, an informal "network of networks" that connects millions of computers at universities, government offices, and private businesses worldwide.

The frenzy over the digital highway came to a full boil early in 1994 when Bell Atlantic, one of the seven Regional Bell Operating Companies (RBOCs), proposed to merge with TCI, the largest cable TV operator in the United States. The on-again, off-again merger negotiations involved several other companies, notably Paramount

Pictures, Blockbuster Video, and QVC, one of the shop-at-home cable TV channels. While the deal was called off at the last minute, the publicity surrounding what would have been the largest merger in U.S. history raised the public's (and Wall Street's) awareness that some major events are happening along the digital highway. It's going to be a heck of a ride.

PART ONE

What's the Big Deal?

BANDWIDTH. THAT'S THE big deal, or at least one of several big deals. What is *bandwidth*? It's the ability of a transmission medium (in this case, a cable) to carry signals—pictures, data, audio, or anything else that can travel over a wire. The higher the bandwidth, the better connected you are. The digital highway is all about increasing the bandwidth between you and the rest of the world.

Back in the 1880s, when Alexander Graham Bell was creating what would become the Bell System, bandwidth wasn't a concern. Fortunately for Bell, the human voice covers a range of about 300 to 2,000 cycles per second—that's 2,000 hertz (Hz), or 2 kilohertz (KHz). That's not much bandwidth, so the Bell System (and most other phone systems worldwide) were built to accommodate only 2 KHz signals. Sounds below 300 Hz and above 2,000 Hz are simply discarded by the telephone network. The limited bandwidth allows telephone circuits to use inexpensive, small-gauge wire. In fact, some early rural telephone circuits used barbed-wire fences as their transmission medium!

Telephone system technology has improved dramatically over the past 100 years, but most of the improvements have been in the switching and routing of calls and in the reliability of the worldwide telephone network. The long-haul network—the part of the network that carries calls between cities, states, and countries—is entirely digital. But in order to maintain compatibility with the hundreds of millions of existing telephones and switchboards, the "last mile" from the phone company to your home or office uses an analog voice signal traveling over a pair of small-gauge copper wires. Analog signals are notoriously susceptible to interference, which is why you sometimes hear buzzes, clicks, and other peoples' conversations on your telephone. See Part 3 of this book for details on analog and digital technology.

For all its shortcomings, analog telephone service has served us well for the past 100 years. It could serve us well for another 100 years, except for two things: bandwidth and capacity.

As you probably know (and as you'll see in detail in Chapter 15), you can use a device called a *modem* to connect your PC to your telephone line. Computers are purely digital devices—they communicate in a binary language consisting simply of "on" (1) and "off" (0). Because the telephone network was designed to carry voice signals, it cannot transport digital data.

A modem gets around this problem by converting the computer's binary zeros and ones into varying tones that can be sent over ordinary telephone lines. The modem at the other end of the line converts the tones back into binary ones and zeros. The speed at which the modems can carry data is limited by the bandwidth of the telephone line.

There's a direct correlation between the telephone line bandwidth and the theoretical maximum modem speed. A few years ago, 2,400 bits per second (bps) was the top speed for personal computer modems. Driven by the explosion in demand for faster, more reliable modems, the modem manufacturers have managed to increase speeds up to about 28,800 bps. Beyond 28,800 bps, however, the laws of physics start to get in the way, and the 3.5 KHz bandwidth limitation becomes a brick wall blocking any further progress.

Of course, speed is relative. If you simply want to move a 1 megabyte (MB) data file from your home to your office, a 28,800 bps modem can do it in about 6 minutes. But if you want to see full-motion, color video with sound on your PC screen, you'll need about 100 times more bandwidth.

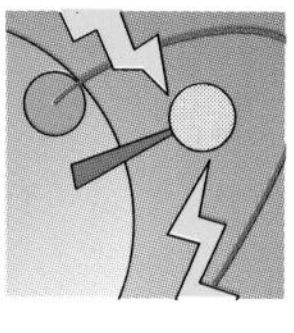

Telephone lines carry one conversation at a time. This means, for example, that if you want to use your modem or receive a fax and talk on the phone at the same time, you'll need two lines. Remember, each phone line runs from your home or office all the way to the nearest telephone company central office. In many cities, there simply isn't enough cable capacity to meet the ever-increasing demand for more telephone lines. In some large cities, there just isn't enough space in existing underground cable conduits to run any more copper wire. As you might expect, creating new underground tunnels in a city like New York or London is a frightfully expensive proposition. Those costs are passed on to the telephone subscribers in the form of higher phone bills.

The cable television systems installed in most U.S. cities don't have a bandwidth problem. In fact, they have bandwidth to spare—enough to carry 250,000 simultaneous telephone conversations (or 9.6 *billion* bps of data)—but they are essentially one-way systems. They're great for bringing large quantities of data into your home or office, and that's exactly what they're designed to do. However, unlike the telephone network, there is no way for you to put a signal back into the cable system's wire for your friend across town to see.

Each telephone subscriber has a discrete pair of wires that connect the subscriber to the phone company's central switching office. Cable systems don't need to have a separate wire for each subscriber. As a result, the cable coming into your home has exactly the same electronic signals on it as the cable going into a friend's home across town. Cable operators can use a variety of methods to block your access to certain channels, but the signal on the cable is the same all over town.

Like the telephone network, cable TV systems are also analog networks. Because cable signals are viewed on standard television receivers, the signal on the TV cable is the same type of analog signal transmitted by over-the-air TV stations.

So, most homes in the United States are wired into two networks: the flexible, but limited-bandwidth dial-telephone network, and the high-bandwidth, one-way, cable TV network. The goal of the digital highway is to combine the bandwidth of the cable network with the switching flexibility of the telephone network. The result will be a two-way, high-bandwidth network that will allow users to send and receive video, voice, and computer data, all on the same wire at the same time. In telecommunications industry jargon, this marriage of technologies (computer, telephone, and video) is called *convergence.*

Convergence has become a big deal in the communications industries (including the telephone, cable TV, broadcasting, and motion-picture production industries) because it has the potential to rearrange everything. When Henry Ford set out to build his automotive empire, he didn't know that Howard Johnson's, Exxon, and the New Jersey Turnpike would be parts of the end result. Guglielmo Marconi and Philo T. Farnsworth, the fathers of radio and television, never could have envisioned "I Love Lucy," Howard Stern, or MTV. Even Thomas Watson, the legendary founder of IBM, couldn't have foreseen the radical changes that computers would bring about—in fields as diverse as medicine, agriculture, and space exploration.

The convergence of television, the computer, and global digital communications likewise will have far-reaching consequences. Some of these are obvious, and some will be pleasant by-products—like Howard Johnson's rum raisin ice cream.

A Current At-home Setup

If there's nothing on TV, you might run out and rent a movie or pop a CD-ROM into your computer. Both of these storage media provide inexpensive transportation of data from one place (the rental store) to another (your TV or PC).

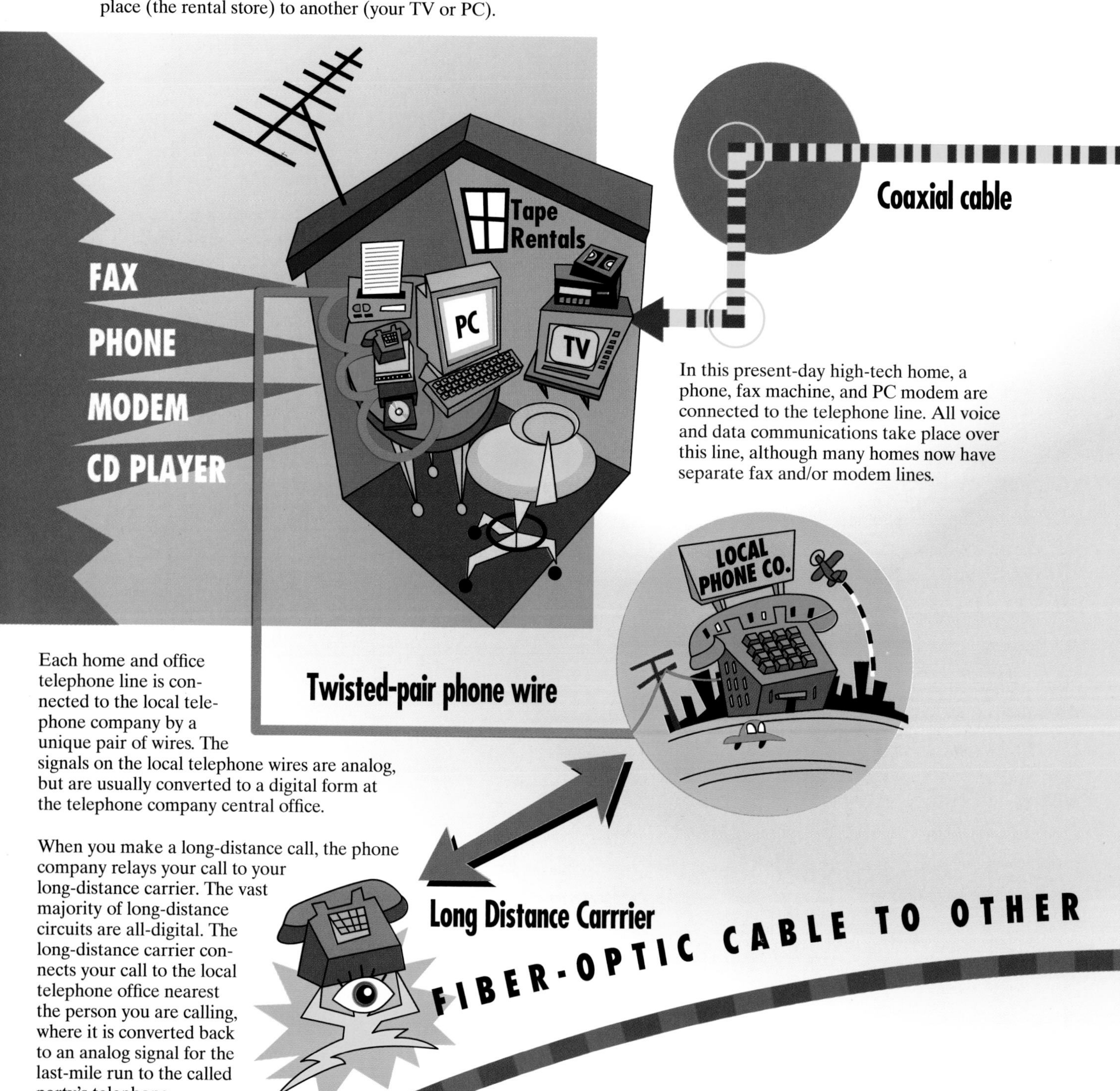

In this present-day high-tech home, a phone, fax machine, and PC modem are connected to the telephone line. All voice and data communications take place over this line, although many homes now have separate fax and/or modem lines.

Each home and office telephone line is connected to the local telephone company by a unique pair of wires. The signals on the local telephone wires are analog, but are usually converted to a digital form at the telephone company central office.

When you make a long-distance call, the phone company relays your call to your long-distance carrier. The vast majority of long-distance circuits are all-digital. The long-distance carrier connects your call to the local telephone office nearest the person you are calling, where it is converted back to an analog signal for the last-mile run to the called party's telephone.

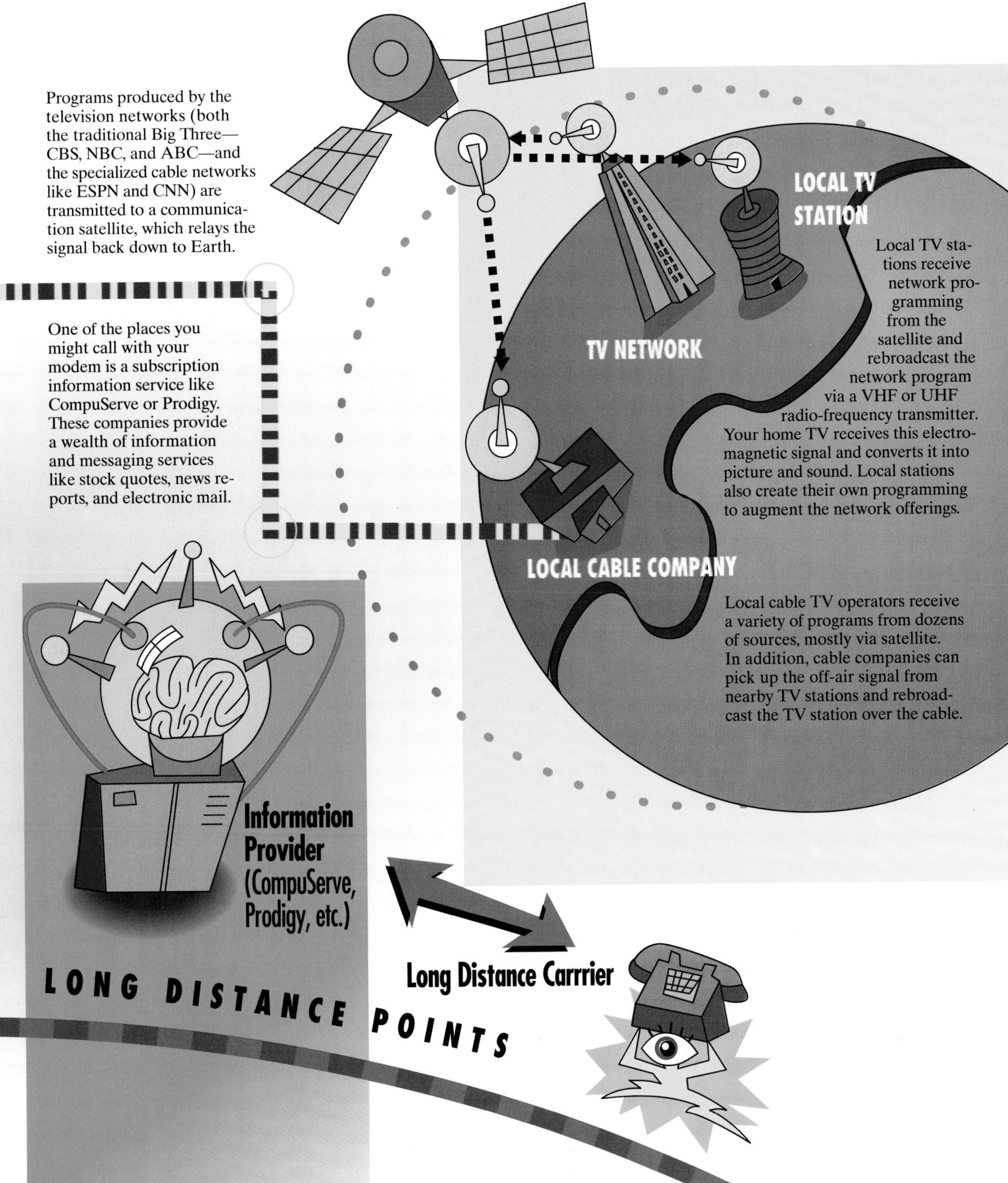
Programs produced by the television networks (both the traditional Big Three—CBS, NBC, and ABC—and the specialized cable networks like ESPN and CNN) are transmitted to a communication satellite, which relays the signal back down to Earth.
LOCAL TV STATION
Local TV stations receive network programming from the satellite and rebroadcast the network program via a VHF or UHF radio-frequency transmitter. Your home TV receives this electromagnetic signal and converts it into picture and sound. Local stations also create their own programming to augment the network offerings.
TV NETWORK
One of the places you might call with your modem is a subscription information service like CompuServe or Prodigy. These companies provide a wealth of information and messaging services like stock quotes, news reports, and electronic mail.
LOCAL CABLE COMPANY
Local cable TV operators receive a variety of programs from dozens of sources, mostly via satellite. In addition, cable companies can pick up the off-air signal from nearby TV stations and rebroadcast the TV station over the cable.
Information Provider (CompuServe, Prodigy, etc.)
Long Distance Carrrier
LONG DISTANCE POINTS

How the Digital Highway Will Work

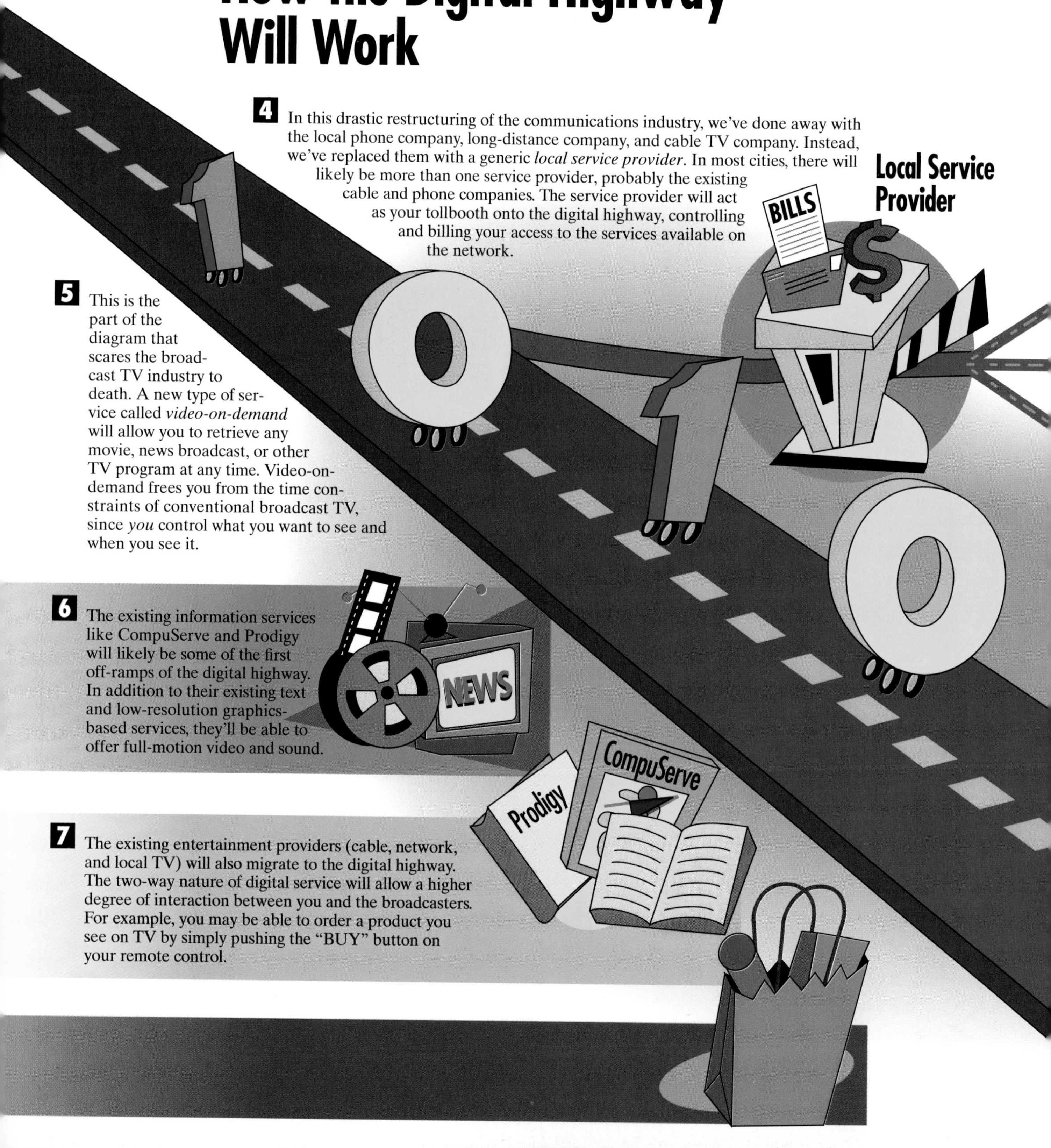

4 In this drastic restructuring of the communications industry, we've done away with the local phone company, long-distance company, and cable TV company. Instead, we've replaced them with a generic *local service provider*. In most cities, there will likely be more than one service provider, probably the existing cable and phone companies. The service provider will act as your tollbooth onto the digital highway, controlling and billing your access to the services available on the network.

Local Service Provider

BILLS

5 This is the part of the diagram that scares the broadcast TV industry to death. A new type of service called *video-on-demand* will allow you to retrieve any movie, news broadcast, or other TV program at any time. Video-on-demand frees you from the time constraints of conventional broadcast TV, since *you* control what you want to see and when you see it.

6 The existing information services like CompuServe and Prodigy will likely be some of the first off-ramps of the digital highway. In addition to their existing text and low-resolution graphics-based services, they'll be able to offer full-motion video and sound.

NEWS

CompuServe

Prodigy

7 The existing entertainment providers (cable, network, and local TV) will also migrate to the digital highway. The two-way nature of digital service will allow a higher degree of interaction between you and the broadcasters. For example, you may be able to order a product you see on TV by simply pushing the "BUY" button on your remote control.

1 In an all-digital world, things will be quite different. You'll still have a phone, PC, and television, but they'll be connected in an entirely different way. Where you formerly had separate cable TV and telephone connections, you'll have a single digital link to the information highway.

3 We've shown a digital VCR atop the television set, but this VCR is actually another computer. It can store the digital data received from the network and can be used to record messages, video clips, or even a personalized video newspaper tailored to your needs.

2 All data entering and leaving your home or office passes through the *premise distribution equipment* (PDE), which is a small computer. The PDE separates the digital signals going to your PC, television, and telephone. Future-generation TVs and PCs will likely have the PDE circuitry built-in.

44600-IOU-$

Money Changes Everything

MONEY, as the saying goes, changes everything. This chapter is about money: how it moves from one place to another, and why it will move differently on the digital highway.

As we saw in Chapter 1, the conversion from analog to digital signaling will change the way we connect our computers, telephones, and televisions to the outside world. Our technological infrastructure has undergone minor technology transitions in the past. For example, at one time most of the switched-telephone network in the United States used rotary dialing. Today, Touch Tone® dialing is the rule, not the exception. Similarly, before the spread of cable TV, every TV set in the United States had an external antenna. When cable TV came along, millions of viewers had to buy new TVs or special converter boxes, or forgo the extra channels that cable offered. But these changes were minor, since the underlying technology of color television and the switched-telephone network remained unchanged.

When it was all over, we didn't use our TVs and phones any differently than we did before the change. We still sat down to watch Walter Cronkite at 6:30 every weeknight, and we still called Aunt Edna in Scottsdale every Sunday afternoon. We still paid our telephone bills, and we still bought products featured by advertisers on TV.

Business on the digital highway will be quite different. Building the digital highway will require huge new investments in equipment at both ends of the highway. And material costs of building the highway itself must be factored in. If we are to move forward into an all-digital era, we'll leave behind a lot of junked equipment that has become obsolete.

At the consumer end of the highway, existing televisions, modems, and VCRs will be entirely incompatible with their newer, digital cousins. As we'll see in Chapter 5, the race is on to build a *set-top box* to facilitate the transition between the analog technology of current-day television and the digital technology of the digital highway.

At the other end of the wire, the information and entertainment providers (television networks, local TV stations, and information services) are faced with a tough choice. They can either shell out vast sums of money to embrace the new technologies, or run the risk of being left behind.

The traditional TV networks will be the hardest pressed here for three reasons. First, the Big Three networks are already under increasing financial pressure due to competition from cable TV and video rentals. There are only so many free hours in a day, and a decreasing part of our nation's free time is spent with ABC, CBS, or NBC. As a result, advertising revenues are in a downward trend. Second, the existing networks have hundreds of affiliate stations who rely on the network for the bulk of their programming. The networks can't risk alienating those affiliate stations; for the near term, those affiliate stations will provide the millions of viewers necessary for advertising-based broadcasting to succeed. Finally, the Big Three networks collectively produce hundreds of hours of new programming each week. Producing the same programming in digital form will require millions of dollars for new equipment.

Then there's the highway itself. The race is on among the nation's regional telephone companies, long-distance carriers, cable TV companies, and even the power companies (they have wires, too) to provide both the high-speed, long-haul "backbone" networks and the local-area "curbside" components of the digital highway. Both will require extraordinary sums of money—by some estimates, as much as $3 trillion. In reality, the digital highway will be a network of interconnected networks, much like today's long-distance telephone network. The enormous cost is simply more than any one company could handle.

Who will pay the huge bill for this conversion? Virtually everyone. Initially, businesses will be the trailblazers and primary users of the digital highway. Businesses aren't interested in 500-channel television, but they are interested in other high-bandwidth pursuits like connecting LANs together and video conferencing.

Fortunately, moving a spreadsheet file from Miami to Seattle is no different than moving a digitized picture from Hollywood to Des Moines. The underlying technology is the same, and it's already in place. Thousands of businesses already use high-speed digital links, and hundreds more come on line every week.

Demand for digital networking services is increasing steadily, and major network providers like AT&T, MCI, and Sprint have been continually adding capacity to their networks. As the network providers add more capacity, the cost of bandwidth comes down. Eventually, bandwidth will become a commodity, and the price of digital service will fall accordingly.

Like most new consumer products, the services on the digital highway are likely to be expensive at first—just as VCRs and personal computers were out of the reach of most consumers in their early days. As more subscribers come on line, and as the digital highway pioneers begin to recoup some of their enormous investments, the prices of services should begin to fall.

Our current local telephone and cable TV services are regulated monopolies. Since there is no competition to keep prices in check, rates for these services are set by the public utilities commission in each state, county, or city. It's quite likely that subscribers in most major cities will have a choice of digital highway service providers—probably the existing telephone and cable TV providers, plus a few start-up companies. This competition should result in lower prices and better service.

As the center of our media universe moves toward the digital highway, we'll see other changes. The two diagrams on the following pages show how our current broadcast, cable, and telephone systems work from a flow-of-money point of view.

Finally, we don't think that advertising-supported TV will go away. Advertising is an important resource, and advertisers are more than willing to underwrite the cost of TV programs to get their message across. We expect that the current TV networks and local TV stations will also find a place on the digital highway as sort of toll-free off-ramps—a place where you can watch all the TV you want as long as you're willing to watch the commercials. In fact, the technology of the digital highway will allow advertisers to target their audiences much more effectively by running different ads to match the viewer household's demographics. Those of you with no young children may never have to watch another disposable diaper commercial again!

How Money Flows Now

In most cities in the United States, customers receive separate bills for their local telephone and long-distance services. But in some areas, the local telephone company bills customers on behalf of the long-distance company, and passes the money on.

Every month, millions of Americans write checks to the phone company, long-distance company, cable TV company, and possibly an information service like CompuServe or America Online. And millions of times each day, people purchase products they've seen on television. This diagram shows where all that money goes.

The Big Three television networks—ABC, CBS, and NBC—collect millions of dollars in advertising revenue each day. Part of that revenue is passed on to the affiliate stations, and part is paid to the program providers who supply the network with their programs. In the past, the networks did much of their own program production. Today, the networks buy most of their programs from outside providers.

If you subscribe to CompuServe, America Online, or another commercial information service, you are billed for the time you spend on the service. Most of these information services offer credit-card billing, saving you from the tedium of writing a check to each service every month.

If you subscribe to cable TV, you pay a fee for basic cable service and an additional fee for premium channels like HBO or Showtime. The cable operator passes part of the fee on to the service provider. In addition, most cable TV companies sell advertising time to local businesses.

As you can see, a network affiliate TV station can be a real money pump. TV stations get much of their revenue from local advertising sales, but they also receive a cut of the network's advertising revenues. In addition, some TV stations collect a fee from cable TV companies that carry their signal. Many TV stations carry syndicated programs, especially in the 7:00 p.m. to 8:00 p.m. time slot before the network begins its evening programming. The local TV station must pay the program syndicator for the rights to that program. Local TV is free for anyone to receive.

Paying for the Digital Highway

Your current telephone or cable TV company will probably be your local service provider. In either case, the service provider will act as your tollbooth onto the digital highway. Instead of receiving a bill from each service you use, you'll receive a single bill (or electronic banking debit) from the service provider.

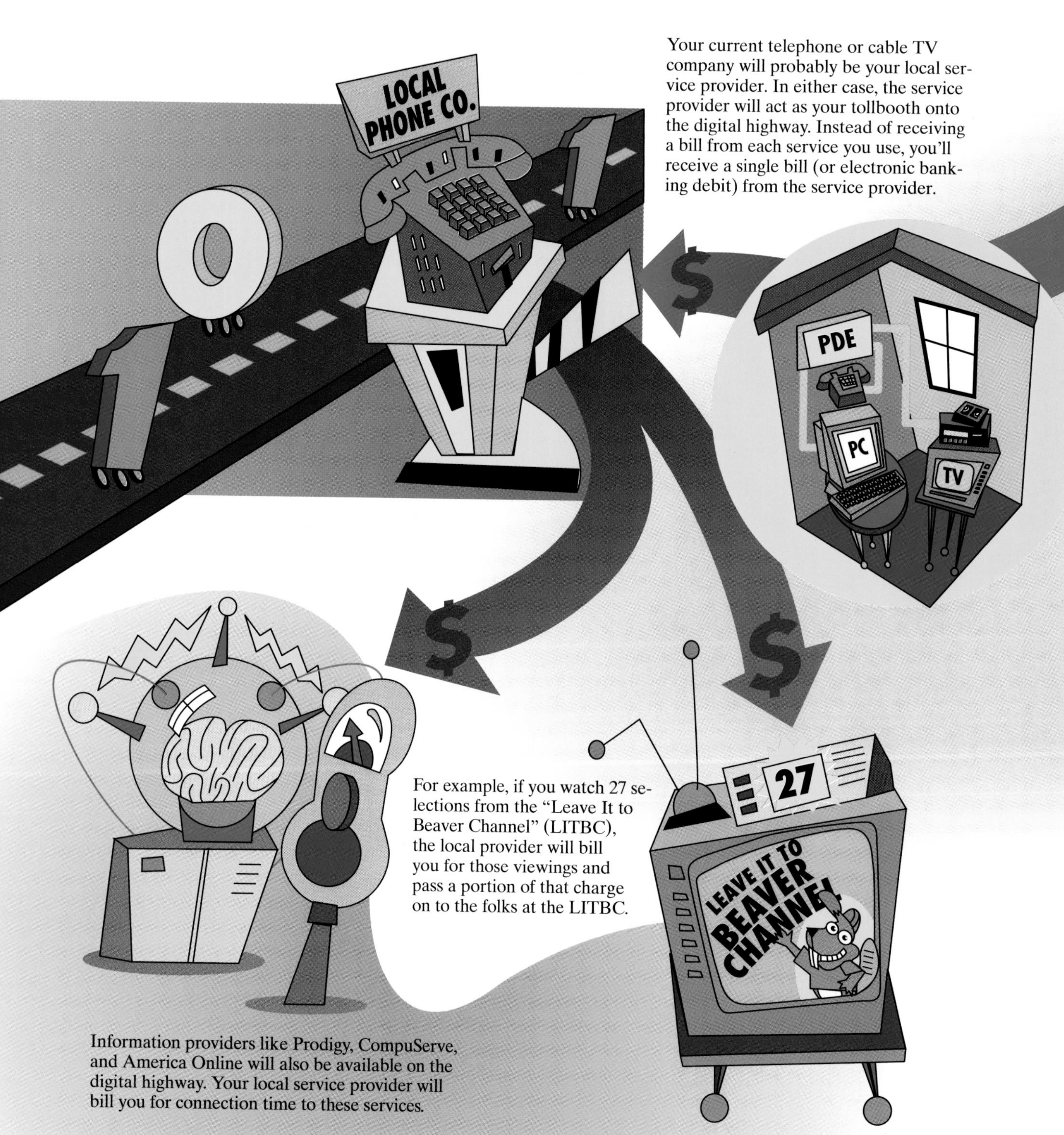

For example, if you watch 27 selections from the "Leave It to Beaver Channel" (LITBC), the local provider will bill you for those viewings and pass a portion of that charge on to the folks at the LITBC.

Information providers like Prodigy, CompuServe, and America Online will also be available on the digital highway. Your local service provider will bill you for connection time to these services.

Advertisers will still buy time on local and network TV, and the TV networks will still buy their programming from outside providers. Local and network TV channels will likely be some of the few free services on the digital highway.

Are We There Yet?

IF YOU'VE EVER taken a long trip with young children, you've heard the question "Are we there yet?" In the case of the digital highway, the answer is...yes and no. A large portion of the digital highway already exists, but we may be years away from completing the necessary exit ramps.

The major national telecommunications carriers—AT&T, MCI, and Sprint—currently provide nationwide and worldwide long-distance voice and data communications services. While our home and office telephones are still 1890s technology analog devices, all but the "last mile" from the local telephone company office to our homes and offices is digital.

In some cases, the last mile is digital, too. Many large office telephone systems are digital; these systems connect to the phone company via a digital service called *T 1*. Recent breakthroughs in video conferencing and in connecting local area networks (LANs) have greatly increased the demand for digital services. But you still can't get T1 service to your home or to a small office; even if you could, it wouldn't be very cost-effective.

The long-distance carriers and local telephone companies have enormous data-carrying capacity on their networks, and they are continually adding additional capacity to meet increased demand. It is this capacity to carry traffic that will form the backbone of the digital highway.

So much for the backbone. Now what about that last mile? Until 1984, one company, AT&T, controlled 90 percent of the telephone service in the United States. In 1983, AT&T agreed to settle a longstanding antitrust suit brought by the U.S. Department of Justice. As part of the settlement, AT&T was split into pieces, with each of the seven Regional Bell Operating Companies (RBOCs) becoming an independent company. Under the terms of the settlement, AT&T can no longer operate local telephone companies. Conversely, the RBOCs are prohibited from carrying interstate long-distance calls.

On January 1, 1984 ("D-Day," for "Divestiture Day"), the entire telecommunications industry changed. Perhaps the most notable change was that AT&T lost control over the industry they created. At one time, AT&T set the standards for the telephone industry. AT&T built, installed, and owned virtually all of the telephone equipment in the United States. After D-Day, they were just another long-distance company and equipment vendor.

As a result of the divestiture, control over the last mile now belongs to the seven RBOCs and the independent telephone companies like Centel and GTE. At one time, adoption of a new standard (like Touch Tone) required nothing more than an edict from AT&T. Today, any technical change requires the close cooperation of the RBOCs and the independent telephone companies.

So, the digital highway runs between all the existing telephone company offices, and then, with a few exceptions, it comes to an abrupt dead end. If the telephone companies are to control the last mile—thus bringing the digital highway to your doorstep—they will need to move quickly and in unison.

While the Bell System was being dismantled, another giant communications industry was being born. Once a loose congregation of CATV (community antenna television) systems, cable TV has become a major industry, reaching nearly 60 percent of all homes. Originally, CATV systems did just what their name implied: They acted as a community antenna. The early cable systems simply put up a tall tower covered with TV antennas, enabling them to pick up broadcast TV signals from nearby cities. They retransmitted these signals over the cable, allowing subscribers to get a clear picture without the inconvenience of an outside antenna. It didn't take long for an industry to blossom. Cable-only networks like HBO and Showtime soon appeared, offering first-run movies to cable viewers.

In the late 1970s, Atlanta businessman Ted Turner put the signal of his TV station, WTBS, up on a satellite. Cable companies nationwide could carry WTBS at very little cost to them, and so the first "super station" was born. Suddenly, his tiny UHF station—an also-ran in the crowded Atlanta TV market—had millions of viewers tuning in to watch old movies, wrestling matches, and Atlanta Braves baseball games.

Millions of viewers translate into millions of advertising dollars. Before long, Turner and other broadcasters started dozens of channels aimed exclusively at cable viewers. Today, there are dozens of specialty channels like MTV, VH-1, Nickelodeon, The Weather Channel, A&E, and Black Entertainment Television.

In order to serve the burgeoning demand for cable TV service, the cable TV operators laid miles of cable. Initially, they used a large-diameter coaxial cable, similar to the cable that connects to your TV set. Coaxial cable loses a good portion of its signal over long runs, so the cable must pass through an electronic amplifier every half-mile or so. Unfortunately, the amplifiers require AC power, making them susceptible to lightning damage and power outages. In addition, each amplifier in the line distorts the signal slightly. In many areas, the original long-haul coaxial cable has been replaced with fiber-optic cable. As we'll see in Chapter 14, fiber-optic cable can cover very long distances without amplifiers. Fiber cable has another advantage: It has a much higher bandwidth than coaxial cable, making it the transport medium of choice for the digital highway.

With all that fiber buried underground and hanging in the air, and with their connections to all the popular entertainment services, the cable companies are in the running to become the primary service providers for the digital highway. But there are downsides, too. Cable is a residential service, so there is no cable service in many all-commercial areas. The cable companies aren't connected to the long-distance carriers, but that can be fixed with a few more miles of fiber-optic cable.

The biggest shortcoming of cable is that it is a one-way service; the cable company can send pictures to you, but you don't get to send anything back to them (other than your monthly payment). This one-way cable is fine for delivering our current day cable programming, but it can't handle the interactive TV of the near future.

Finally, the topography of cable is radically different than that of the telephone network. Because it's designed to be a one-way system, there's no switching or by-the-minute billing system in place.

So who will provide your access to the digital highway? Your local phone company, your cable company, and probably a third provider offering wireless technology. So tell the kids to relax—we're almost there.

Subscriber Equipment

Every individual telephone line is a dedicated pair of wires all the way from the wall jack to the telephone company office. Typically, each telephone line travels individually to a neighborhood's or office's subscriber line interface carrier (SLIC), where the line is spliced into a thicker cable with dozens or hundreds of other lines. In some areas, the thick trunk cable has been replaced with fiber-optic cable.

Traffic between the local telephone company and the long-distance companies is also digital, usually utilizing T1- or T3-class connections.

From the SLIC, individual telephone lines travel over small-gauge copper wire to individual homes and offices. This wire is either buried underground or strung overhead, making it very difficult to replace.

Large commercial telephone users can order digital T1 or T3 service. Each T1 circuit provides the equivalent of 24 voice circuits. T1 and T3 can travel over copper or fiber-optic cabling.

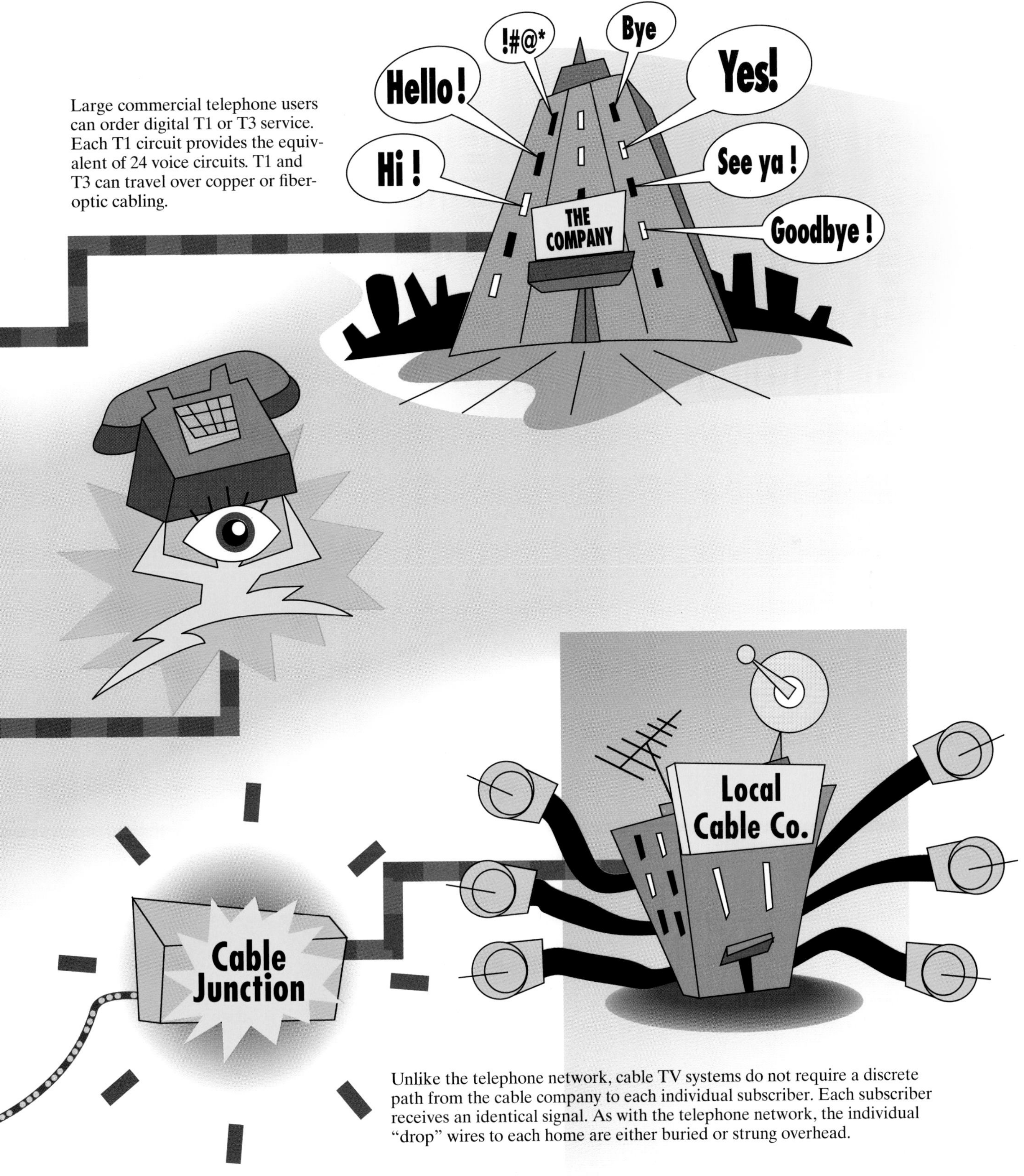

Unlike the telephone network, cable TV systems do not require a discrete path from the cable company to each individual subscriber. Each subscriber receives an identical signal. As with the telephone network, the individual "drop" wires to each home are either buried or strung overhead.

PART

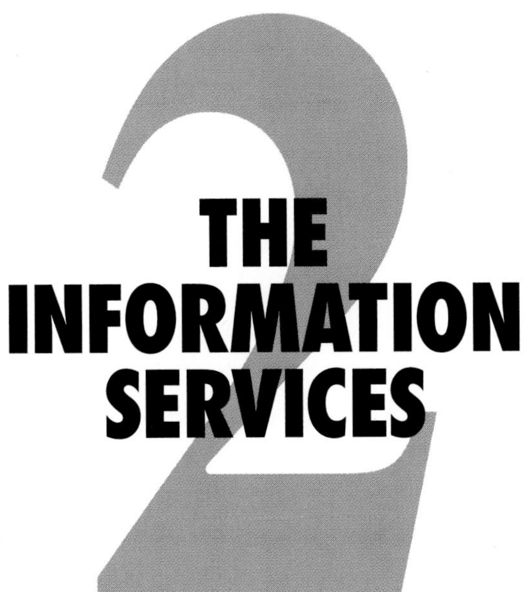

THE INFORMATION SERVICES

WHEN PRESENTED WITH a new technology such as the digital highway, most people ask, "What's in it for me?" The next nine chapters answer that question.

First, let us tell you what the digital highway *isn't* going to be. Despite what you've heard, it's not going to be 500-channel television. It's not going to be George Jetson's wall-sized two-way TV, and it's not going to be the all-seeing, all-knowing government television seen in *Brazil* and George Orwell's *1984*.

Now, here are some of the plans the federal government has for getting the digital highway project off the ground. Yes, part of the plan calls for something called "video-on-demand." Yes, there are plans for interactive television. Video-on-demand and interactive television top the "sure bets" list for home use (both are discussed in Chapter 6). In the business world, the digital highway will bring inexpensive LAN linking and video conferencing to even the smallest businesses. You are also likely to see some new services that weren't possible before.

Some existing services like electronic mail and on-line information services are ideally suited for the digital highway. Currently the province of the computer cognescenti, services like MCI Mail, CompuServe, and Prodigy will be able to extend their reach to the millions of people who don't own a computer. The services themselves will be faster and more convenient to use. Full-motion video and hi-fi sound will replace the low-resolution graphics and plain text now used by on-line services.

What about 500-channel television? We don't think consumers are willing to pay what it would cost. We pay about $40 per month for "basic plus" cable. Here in our part of Florida, as in most areas, basic plus means that you get all the local TV stations, a few cable channels like MTV, The Weather Channel, A&E, TBS, CNN, and a few others—about 24 channels. The local cable operator pays a per-subscriber fee to the program providers for each of those channels—as much as $1 per channel per month—so each additional channel costs the cable operator money. Five hundred channels (20.83 times our existing 24 channels) would work out to be about $830 per month!

Even if the numbers worked out, it's doubtful that the TV industry could come up with enough programming to fill 500 channels anyway. If you've ever channel-surfed your cable TV with your remote control, you know that there's precious little good programming outside of prime time. (Some folks would argue that there's not much on during prime time, either. As Bruce Springsteen lamented, there are "Fifty-seven channels and there's nothin' on.")

The reason for the lack of good programming is simple: It costs big money. High-quality programming can cost upwards of $1 million per hour to produce. The networks make money on programs by selling advertising time; the larger the audience, the higher the ad rates. Even after 50 years of experience, the networks still roll the dice every time they produce a new program. If the program's audience doesn't materialize as planned, advertisers stay away, and the network loses money.

So instead of 500 channels, what you will see is plenty of programming offered on-demand. If you want to see "Lonesome Dove" or "The Hitchhiker's Guide to the Galaxy" or even your three favorite episodes of "I Love Lucy" at 3:00 a.m., they'll be available to you. Video-on-demand will allow program producers to recoup their investment over many years, rather than hoping for a one-time big hit. It will also allow consumers to choose what they want to see, when they want to see it.

Two-way video telephones? For some business uses (namely, video conferencing), yes. In fact, video conferencing is already beginning to catch on in the business world. Two-way video conferencing needs plenty of bandwidth. When bandwidth was expensive, so was conferencing. Before the availability of on-demand digital links, video conference calls had to be scheduled days in advance. In most cases, it was simpler, faster, and often cheaper to fly the parties involved to one place for a meeting. Today, video conference calls can be set up in seconds, and the cost is far less than the price of a few plane tickets. There's a huge time savings, too. With video conferencing, the parties involved can get together with no time lost traveling. On a video conference call, your plane can't get snowed in, and there are no airport hot dogs or lost luggage. With travel costs rising and bandwidth costs dropping, we can expect to see a continued boom in business video conferencing.

As for two-way video telephones in the home, forget it. AT&T has been trying to push video telephones for 30 years; the first video telephone (the AT&T Picturephone) made its debut at the 1964 World's Fair. But people don't necessarily want to be seen while they're talking on the telephone. Part of what we've come to know as "talking on the telephone" is the exchange of verbal ideas with another disembodied voice. When you throw a live picture into the equation, things change. Facial expressions, body language, and other visual clues become part of the conversation. That's not talking on the telephone as we are accustomed to it, and it makes many people uncomfortable.

The digital highway will also make government more accessible to you. In fact, that goal is part of the National Information Infrastructure (NII) plan of action: "The Administration will seek to ensure that Federal agencies, in concert with state and local governments, use the NII to expand the information available to the public, ensuring that the immense reservoir of government information is available to the public easily and equitably."

While some of that "immense reservoir of government information" is extremely boring, other parts are downright exciting. Imagine being able to look up and retrieve historical documents from the Library of Congress, or take a video tour of the Smithsonian, right from your personal computer or television.

Some of that government information is already available directly from the government via the Internet computer network. For example, the above quote from the NII Agenda was extracted from the actual NII Agenda for Action document. It only took a few seconds to get it and didn't cost a cent. Virtually all government agencies are already on the Internet, and more information is available from this source every day. We'll look at the Internet in more detail in Chapter 9.

As we've already seen in Chapter 2, the digital highway must stand on its own financial feet. So what is the financial basis for the government's involvement in the digital highway anyway? Again, we quote the NII Agenda: "Because information means empowerment—and employment—the government has a duty to ensure that all Americans have access to the resources and job creation potential of the Information Age."

That's what's in it for you.

PART TWO

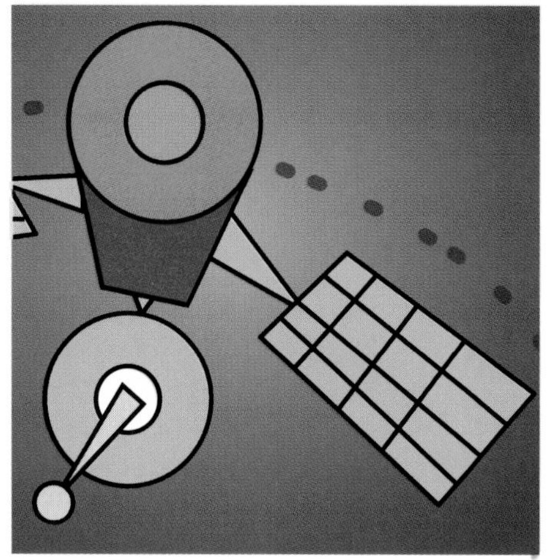

Our Media Infrastructure

BEFORE WE EXPLAIN (in Chapters 5 and 6) how the digital highway will change our media infrastructure, we thought it might be helpful to show how the existing structure works. Since the 1920s, our media infrastructure has grown from a handful of radio stations to a major industry. There are thousands of radio, TV, and cable TV outlets in the United States, and thousands more overseas.

While there have been many advances in broadcast technology over the years, the basic concept has remained the same: A broadcaster sends out a signal which is received by an audience. Everyone in the audience gets the same signal at the same time. This model dates back to the early days of radio, and it underlies the one-way nature of broadcasting. Cable TV follows this same model; everyone on the cable system gets the same signal.

All our existing video media (broadcast TV, network TV, cable, and videotape) are based on a rigid business hierarchy that essentially grants some intermediary (the TV networks, cable operators, or video rental stores) a guaranteed piece of the entertainment pie. Program producers (the motion picture studios, independent filmmakers, and TV program producers) can only sell their products to one of a few video media outlets—either broadcast or cable TV, or the retail videotape market. There's simply no way to get a TV show, movie, or documentary film to the masses without first selling the product to one of these outlets.

Because there are a limited number of radio, TV, and cable channels, broadcasters make choices for us. They decide what programs we want to see, and what time of the day we want to see them. Since most of our TV is supported by advertising, these decisions are based entirely on ratings—the more viewers, the higher the advertising revenues. The result of this process is that all the decisions are based on the ratings. Quality and content aren't as important as good Nielsen ratings.

Most of the major innovations in mass media have capitalized on the role that time plays in this industry. For example, live television provides an immediacy (especially in coverage of major news events) that newspapers can never achieve. Before television, the nation's newspapers were our primary source of news. The papers flourished, and most major cities had two or three daily newspapers. Once TV took hold, the newspapers found themselves hurting. TV cut into advertising revenues, and hundreds of newspapers went bankrupt during the 1970s and '80s.

Similarly, CNN and entertainment networks like HBO provide viewers with news and movies free of the time constraints of broadcast TV. The free-form architecture of the digital highway will further release us from the tyranny of time by allowing us to choose from a vast repertoire of programming, at any time of day.

Failing to learn a lesson from their newspaper cousins, the TV networks laughed at TV pioneer Ted Turner when he announced that he was starting an all-news cable network in 1980. They're not laughing anymore. Turner's CNN and sister station Headline News have put a noticeable dent in the major networks' evening news audience. CNN and Headline News are on the air 24 hours a day, so news-hungry viewers no longer have to wait for the Big Three network news broadcasts. As we pointed out earlier, ratings mean money, and CNN has cost the networks plenty. CNN and other cable news sources haven't put the Big Three out of business, but they've made them sit up and take notice.

The video rental stores are concerned about these trends, too. The major advantage of videotape is that it allows the viewer to watch a movie free of the time constraints of broadcast TV and theaters. When you rent a movie on tape, you can watch that movie when you want, as often as you want. If the phone rings, you can stop the tape and restart it later. If you miss a scene, you can rewind the tape and watch the scene again. Consumers love tape rentals, and the tape-rental business has grown from a handful of mom-and-pop stores to a major industry. But, if you could order any movie (including first-run features) at any time, without having to leave the house, why would you go to video store?

It's clear that the digital highway will alter the existing order of the consumer interface with the media, and vice versa. As we'll see in the next few chapters, we're about to see a shoot-out in the media corral.

How Broadcast TV Works

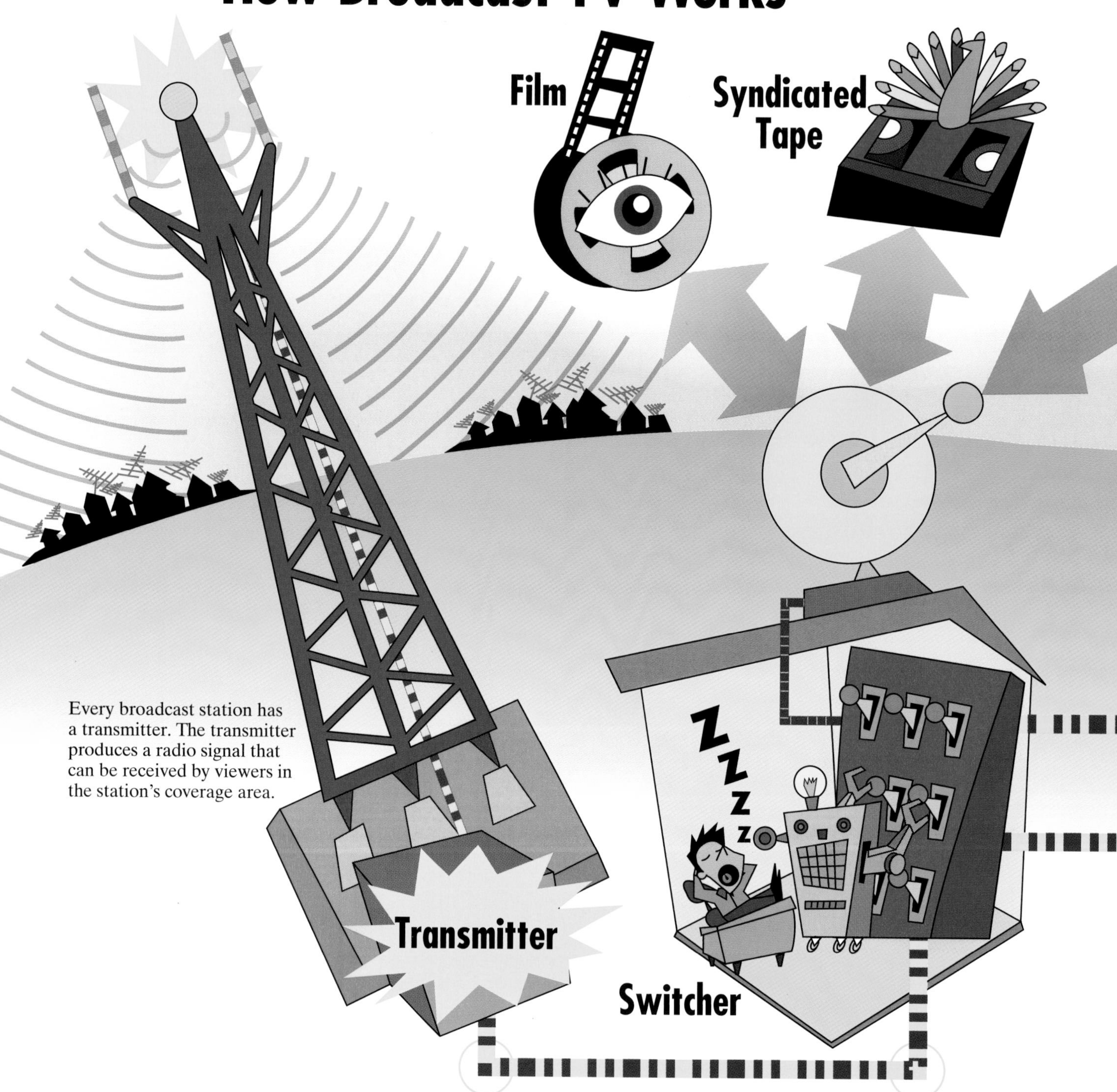

Every broadcast station has a transmitter. The transmitter produces a radio signal that can be received by viewers in the station's coverage area.

At the heart of every TV station is the *on-air switcher*. This electronic switch connects to virtually everything else in the station and allows the switch operator to control what goes out over the air. In many stations, the on-air switcher is operated by a computer, with a human operator watching over it.

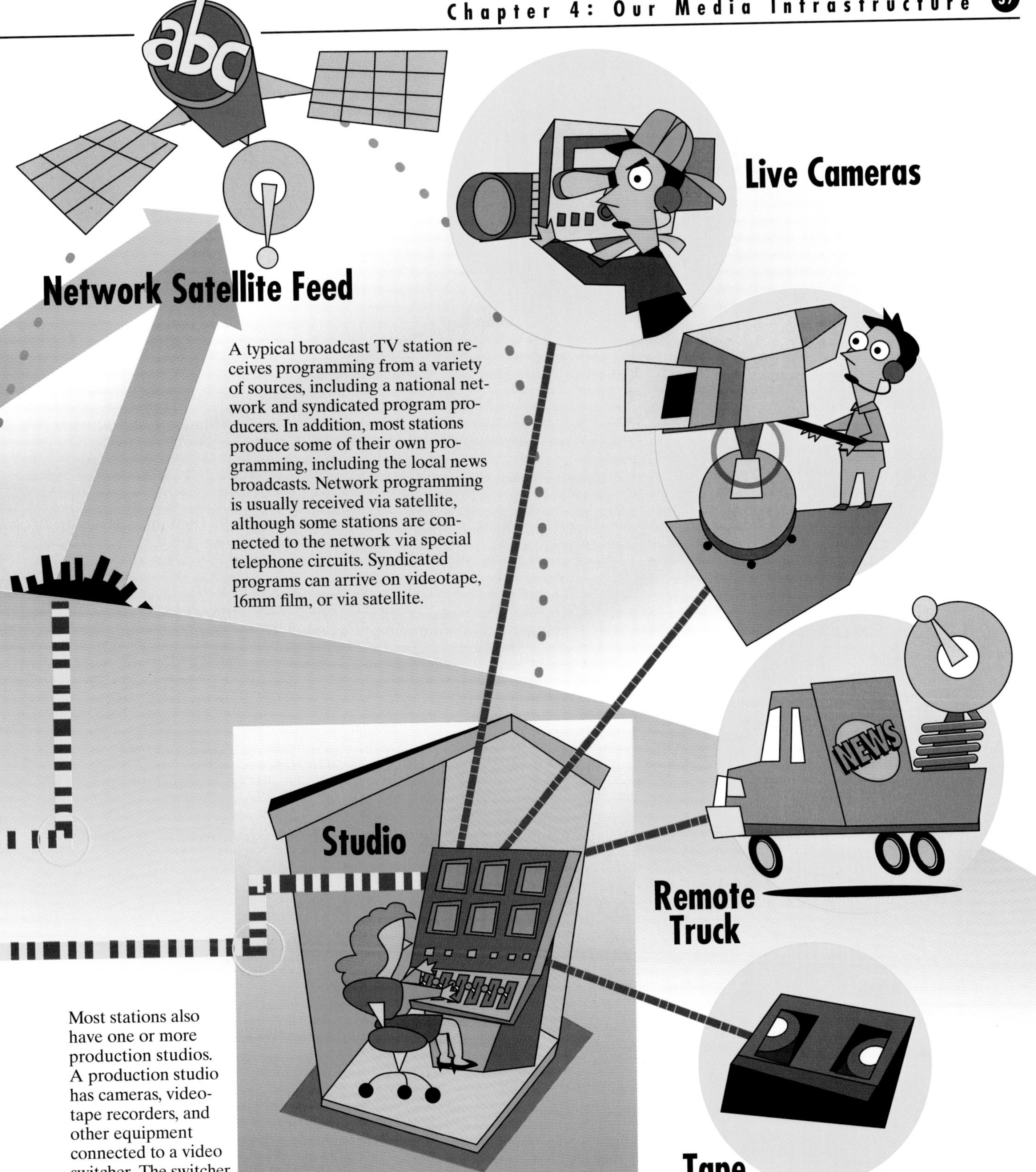

A typical broadcast TV station receives programming from a variety of sources, including a national network and syndicated program producers. In addition, most stations produce some of their own programming, including the local news broadcasts. Network programming is usually received via satellite, although some stations are connected to the network via special telephone circuits. Syndicated programs can arrive on videotape, 16mm film, or via satellite.

Most stations also have one or more production studios. A production studio has cameras, videotape recorders, and other equipment connected to a video switcher. The switcher allows the producer or director to decide which video source (camera, videotape, and so on) the viewers will see at any point in the program. The output from the studio can be fed live to the on-air switcher or can be routed to a videotape recorder for later playback.

How Network TV Works

Like local TV stations, the national TV networks take signals from a variety of sources and retransmit them. Also like local TV stations, the networks have a central on-air switcher. The switcher operator can select any of dozens of studios, videotape machines, and satellite receivers.

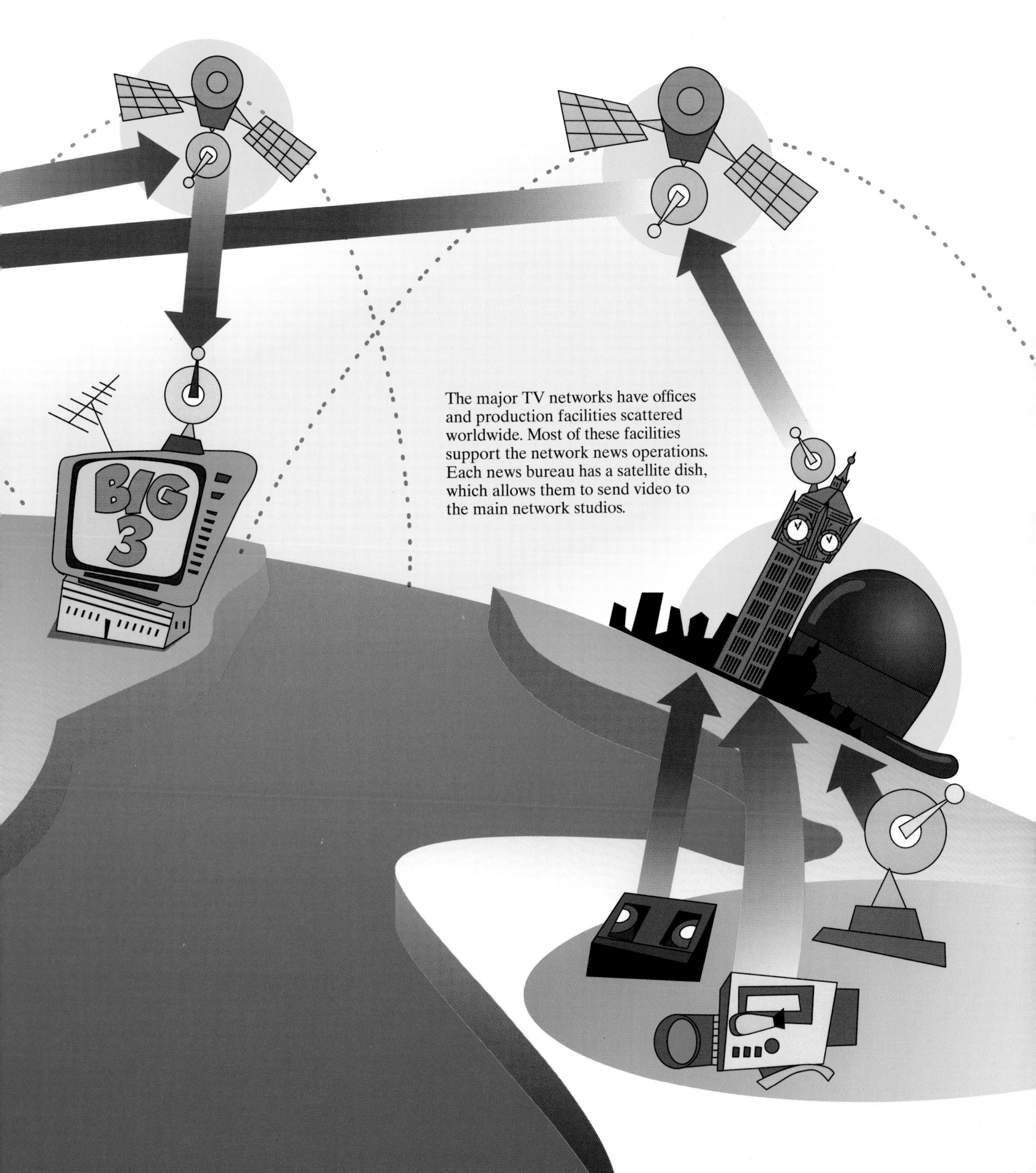

The major TV networks have offices and production facilities scattered worldwide. Most of these facilities support the network news operations. Each news bureau has a satellite dish, which allows them to send video to the main network studios.

How Cable TV Works

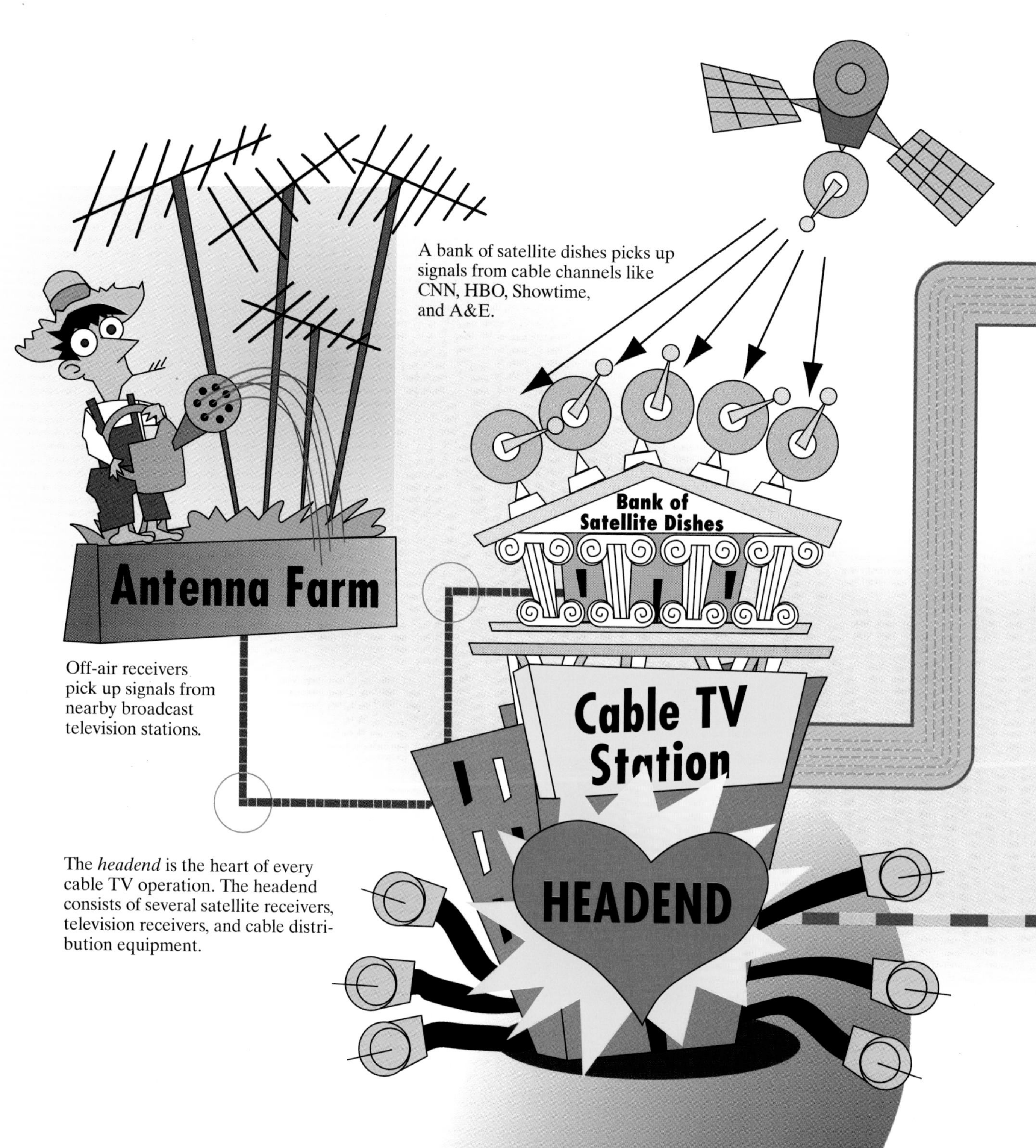

A bank of satellite dishes picks up signals from cable channels like CNN, HBO, Showtime, and A&E.

Off-air receivers pick up signals from nearby broadcast television stations.

The *headend* is the heart of every cable TV operation. The headend consists of several satellite receivers, television receivers, and cable distribution equipment.

Each signal received by the headend is transmitted on a separate channel. A device called a *modulator* takes each video source and assigns it one of the cable system's channels. The outputs of all the modulators feed into a *combiner*, which puts all the channels together on one cable.

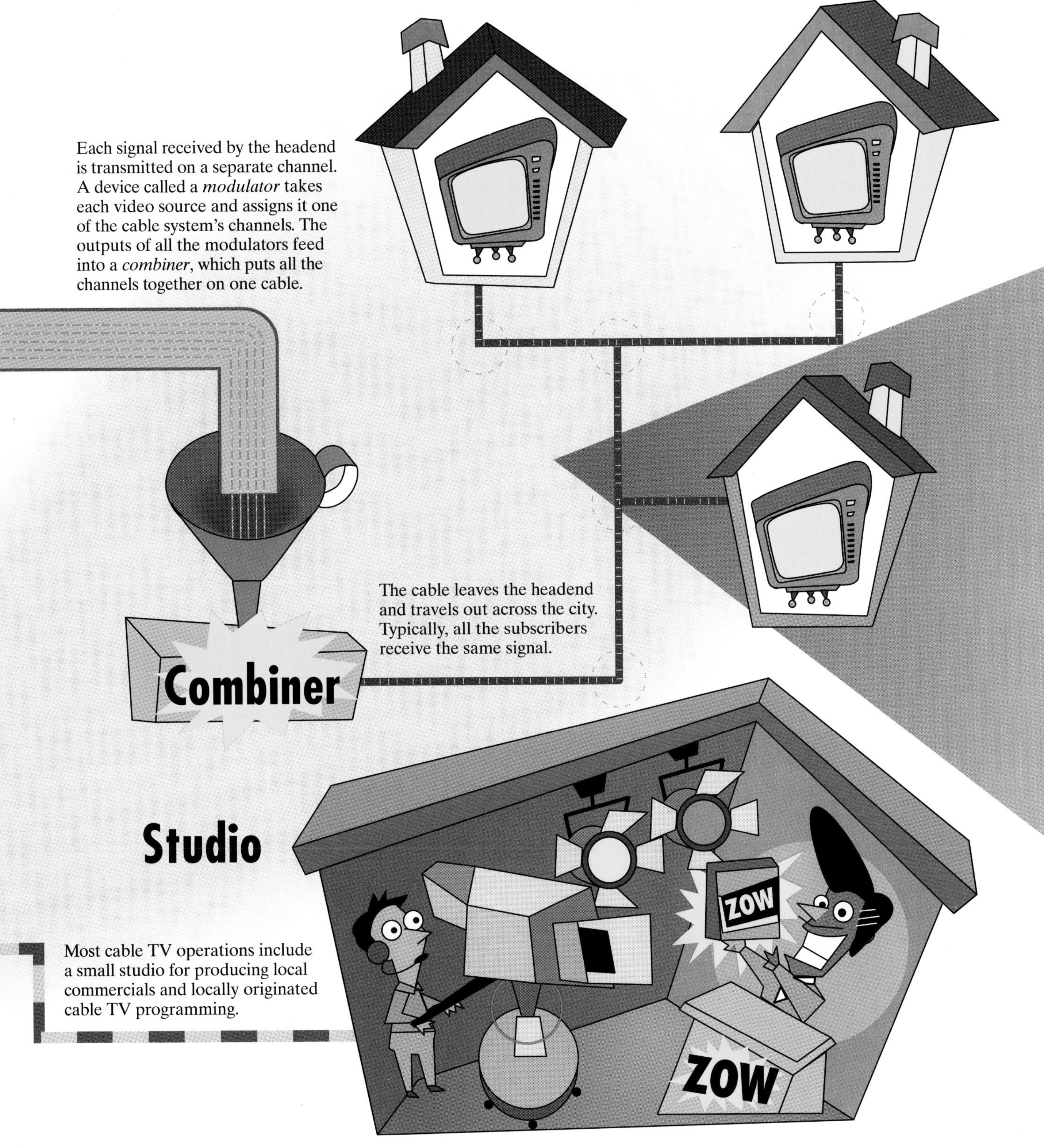

The cable leaves the headend and travels out across the city. Typically, all the subscribers receive the same signal.

Most cable TV operations include a small studio for producing local commercials and locally originated cable TV programming.

148837

What's a Set-Top Box?

A SET-TOP BOX is a cable TV box. It's a computer (maybe more powerful than your desktop PC). It can be a telephone jack, a digital modem, an answering machine, or a fax interface. It can be all of the above.

If you subscribe to cable TV, you may already have a cable TV converter box. That box connects your TV set to the cable TV system. The digital highway's new-generation set-top box has a few things in common with its cable TV cousin, so we'll explain the old before we move on to the new.

Set-top boxes were necessary in the early days of cable because cable companies offered more channels than most TV sets could handle. With these old-style boxes, you set your TV to channel 3 or 4 and left it there. To change channels, you used the channel selector on the cable box. When you selected a channel, the converter box converted that channel to the proper frequency for channel 3 or 4.

Today, all TV sets sold in the United States are *cable-ready*, meaning they can receive all cable channels without the aid of a cable box. A new generation of set-top cable boxes has appeared, but these do more than convert channels. These new boxes are called *addressable converters*, and they allow the cable company to control your cable service from the cable headend. These boxes allow the cable system operator to send out premium (extra charge) channels in a scrambled form, thus preventing cable theft. They also enable a relatively new service called *pay-per-view*.

For example, let's say you're a basic cable subscriber. You get 20 or 30 channels of TV, but the premium channels you don't subscribe to appear on the screen as scrambled hash. One day, your kids convince you that they simply can't live another day without the Disney Channel. So, you call the cable company and tell them that you want to subscribe to it. Five minutes later, one of those formerly scrambled channels clears, and the Disney Channel appears. All it takes is having a technician at the cable headend send a signal out to enable the Disney Channel on your set-top box. All the set-top boxes on the cable network received the same signal, but only your box responded to the message. You're happy because the kids are off watching "Winnie the Pooh," and the cable company is happy because they didn't have to send a technician to your house—but they still got to charge you a $20 "connection fee."

Pay-per-view works similarly. You call and order a pay-per-view event—often a first-run movie, prize fight, or rock concert—and the cable company enables the pay-per-view channel on your box for the duration of the event. After the event, the pay-per-view channel reverts to hash.

Cable companies like set-top boxes because they own them and you have to rent them—just like the old days when all phones were owned by the Bell System. Consumers hate set-top boxes, because they render useless the remote control that comes with most TVs. They also complicate taping of programs because you must remember to set the cable box to the proper channel ahead of time.

The next-generation of the set-top box will be quite different. Its primary role will again be one of converting signals—this time from digital to analog. You see, all the analog electronic stuff you already own (TV, VCR, telephones, modems) will be incompatible with the digital highway. Fortunately, the promoters of the digital highway—the cable systems, phone companies, and service providers—don't expect you to throw away your 41-inch TV or your $300 cordless phone. They want to keep the price of admission to the digital world as low as possible. So, you'll need a set-top box to interface the analog equipment you already own to the digital highway. See Part 3, "Toward a Digital World," for details.

This sounds much easier than it is, and the set-top boxes won't come cheap. Converting a broadcast-quality TV picture from digital to analog requires a whopping amount of computing horsepower. It will also require a good bit of software expertise. Not surprisingly, some of the first set-top box proposals and prototypes have come from computer and software companies.

There are several issues involved with the set-top box, and each bears exploring. The issues concern price, ease of use, compatibility, and standards.

Price may be the most important factor. If the price of admission is too high, most people will stick with their old, analog telephone and cable TV. One of the major points of the NII Agenda for Action states that the project should "Extend the 'universal service' concept to ensure that information resources are available to all at affordable prices."

Ease of use is another of the major issues. Ideally, the box should sit quietly in the background, processing incoming data and performing conversion tasks. But the box also needs to be sophisticated enough to allow data entry—at least enough to be able to type an e-mail letter or navigate through an on-line information service.

Compatibility is the third major issue. The box must be able to convert digital signals to analog so that we can salvage our present-day TVs, telephones, and fax machines. At the same time, the box must be flexible, allowing for software and hardware upgrades to allow connecting all-digital equipment at some point in the future.

The final issue, standards, may be the toughest problem to solve. Just like the early days of the PC industry, there are no standards for set-top boxes. Each set-top box vendor has an agenda, and each would like to have a head start. As usual, the cable system operators see things one way and the telephone companies another. But they both agree that they don't want to be stuck with millions of incompatible boxes a few years down the road. They want to see a nationwide standard adopted very soon, as does the government.

Getting Off and On the Highway

In most homes, the primary use of the set-top box will be to convert incoming digital video to a format that your existing TV and VCR can use. Most newer TV sets can accept direct video inputs; this is the best way to get a high-quality picture.

Most boxes will provide a digital interface connection, allowing you to connect your personal computer to the box. You can then use the digital network to connect your personal computer to information services like Prodigy and CompuServe, but at much higher speeds than today's analog modems provide.

While the exact contents of the box vary from one maker to another, virtually all contain a high-powered CPU chip and plenty of RAM (random access memory), similar to those found in desktop computers. The program code (the actual computer instructions that tell the box what to do) is stored in RAM. If your set-top box ever needs a software update, the service provider can download the new software directly to your box over the network.

In most cases, you'll get your digital service from either your telephone company or your cable TV company. Since the basic digital highway service will likely include telephone and television on the same wire, you won't need both companies anymore. The set-top box will provide telephone service and allow you to connect your existing telephone and fax machine to the digital network.

The set-top box connects the digital highway to an otherwise analog world. The set-top box connects to the digital network, and the rest of your equipment (phone, TV, PC, and so on) connects to the box.

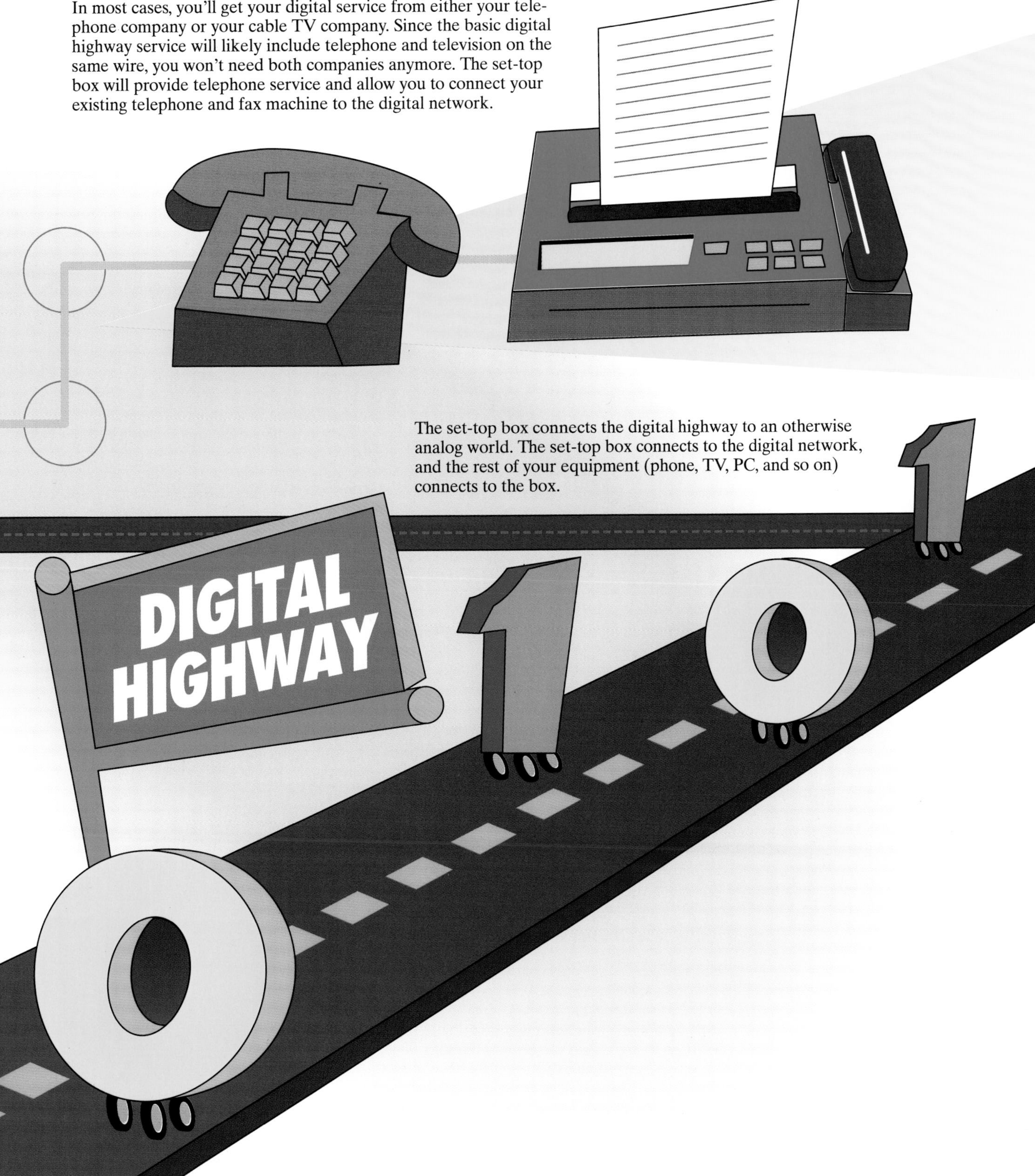

Video-on-Demand and Interactive TV

WE'VE READ HUNDREDS of newspaper and magazine articles touting the imminent arrival of 500-channel television. We're here to tell you that there won't be any such thing. As we pointed out earlier, there's no financial basis for 500-channel TV. We even detected some backlash against the entire concept. The premise is that access to 500 channels will turn everyone in the United States into TV-addicted, channel-surfing couch potatoes, glued to their sets watching Home Shopping Network VII, Australian rules football, or something equally incomprehensible.

What we *will* have is something called video-on-demand. Video-on-demand and interactive TV promise to be two of the most exciting and useful consumer electronic services ever conceived.

Imagine that you have access to a vast library of movies, old television shows, educational videos, documentaries, cartoons, historic events on video, and special-interest programs. Imagine further that you can pick up your remote control, punch in a few commands, and see a menu of all the movies starring, for example, Steve Martin. Punch a few more buttons, and *Roxanne* begins playing on your screen. You didn't have to go to the video store, you don't have to return the tape (rewound, please) to the rental store, and you didn't have to wait for the movie to start. You'll have to pay a few bucks for the privilege—and you'll have to make your own popcorn. Welcome to video-on-demand.

Where will all the programming for video-on-demand come from? From anyone who has programming to sell. As we pointed out in Chapter 2, the digital highway changes all the rules. Program producers will be able to sell the wares directly to the public for the first time. Want first-run movies? Dial up the First-Run Movie Channel, and take your pick of the top 100 current releases. Want old movies? Turner Entertainment has tons of them—just dial up TNT Online. Missed the Braves game last night? No problem—just dial up Sports Unlimited, and you can see any Braves game back to 1976. Of course, we've made up the names of these services, since they're not available yet. But test projects are already up and running, and it won't be long before many services like our examples are available nationwide.

The nation's program producers collectively own millions of hours of programming—everything from old "Barney Miller" shows to news coverage of the Apollo moon landing to last night's

"Nightline." With our current broadcasting system, there's no way for them to make any money off this material. Sure, some of it is available on videotape, but unless you're a hard-core "Bonanza" fan, you're not going to plunk down $20 for a tape you'll watch only once. Once this material is available on-line, you'll be able to choose from a vast library of material. The program owners will make some money, and you'll have more viewing options.

Old movies are fine, but what about new stuff? This is where the "500-channel" concept comes into play. Starting a new video-on-demand service is much simpler than starting a new broadcast or cable TV network. You'll still need a source of programming material, but you won't need much equipment or staff. You also won't need any affiliate stations or cable operators. What you will need is a device called a video server.

If you're familiar with computer networking, you know that a server is a computer system that provides some type of service for users on the network. File servers hold files, print servers manage shared network printers, and communication servers provide shared communications services to the network. A *video server* connects to a network (in this case, the digital highway), and provides digital video and sound to users on the network. The program material resides on the server in digital form—as files on a hard disk, optical disk, or digital tape. In essence, a video server is a specialized file server. When a user requests a particular program, the server retrieves the file containing the digital image and sound, and sends the data out over the network. Like a file server, several users can retrieve files at the same time. Several users can even retrieve the same file at the same time—a feat that videotape can't perform.

Because the barriers to entry are fairly low, we can expect to see hundreds of specialized services available on line. For example, let's say that you're ABC. You know that millions more people would watch "Nightline" if it didn't come on so late. You set up a video server with the prior night's "Nightline," and viewers can tune in at any time. Similar video-on-demand services could provide all types of news, information, and entertainment services.

Five hundred channels is a nice, round number, and it sounds impressive. It has certainly grabbed the public's attention, but the actual number of services on the digital highway may very well exceed 500. Stay tuned!

So much for video-on-demand. Now, what about interactive TV? Interactive television uses a two-way conduit to create an interaction between broadcaster and viewer (or among many viewers). This conduit will be facilitated by the digital highway, which is a two-way street. Our current broadcast media (television, cable, and newspapers) are one-way conduits.

Some very talented folks in the entertainment side of the telecommunications industry think that interactive television will be the killer app that makes us all want to run out and sign up for digital highway service immediately. A *killer app* (app is short for application program) is, in computer industry jargon, a piece of software that makes hardware sell like hotcakes. VisiCalc was the first small computer spreadsheet that became the first-ever killer app. Legend has it that customers would walk into ComputerLand (one of the first computer retail chains) and ask the salesperson for a "VisiCalc Machine."

Years after VisiCalc's success, Aldus Corporation's PageMaker became the killer app that allowed Apple's Macintosh system to revolutionize the printing and typesetting industries. Lotus Development Corporation's 1-2-3 and WordPerfect Corporation's WordPerfect became major killer apps following the introduction of the original IBM PC in 1981. No one knows what the digital highway's killer app will be, but there's a huge pot of gold at the end of the digital rainbow.

Ordering a Video-on-Demand Service

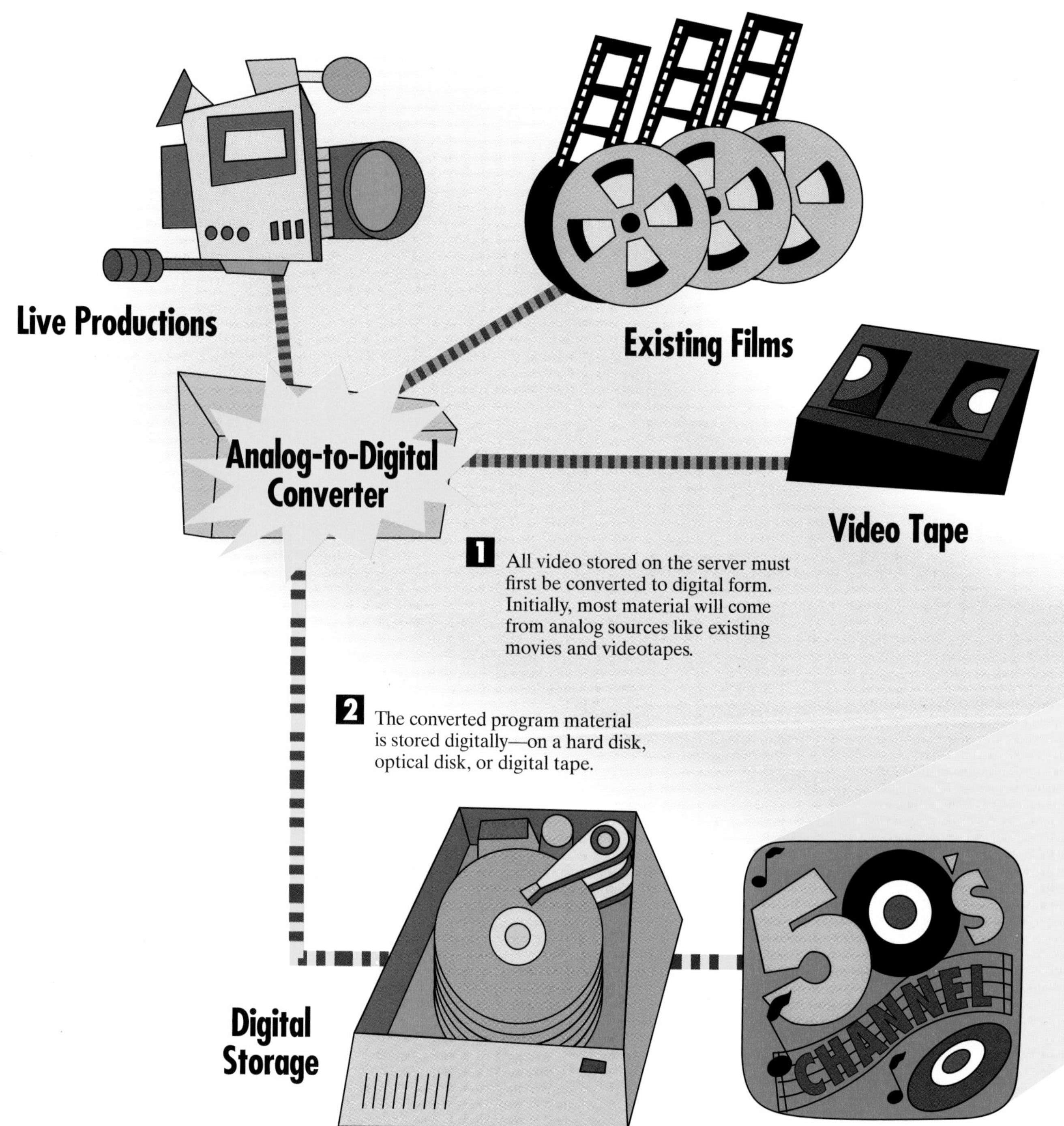

1 All video stored on the server must first be converted to digital form. Initially, most material will come from analog sources like existing movies and videotapes.

2 The converted program material is stored digitally—on a hard disk, optical disk, or digital tape.

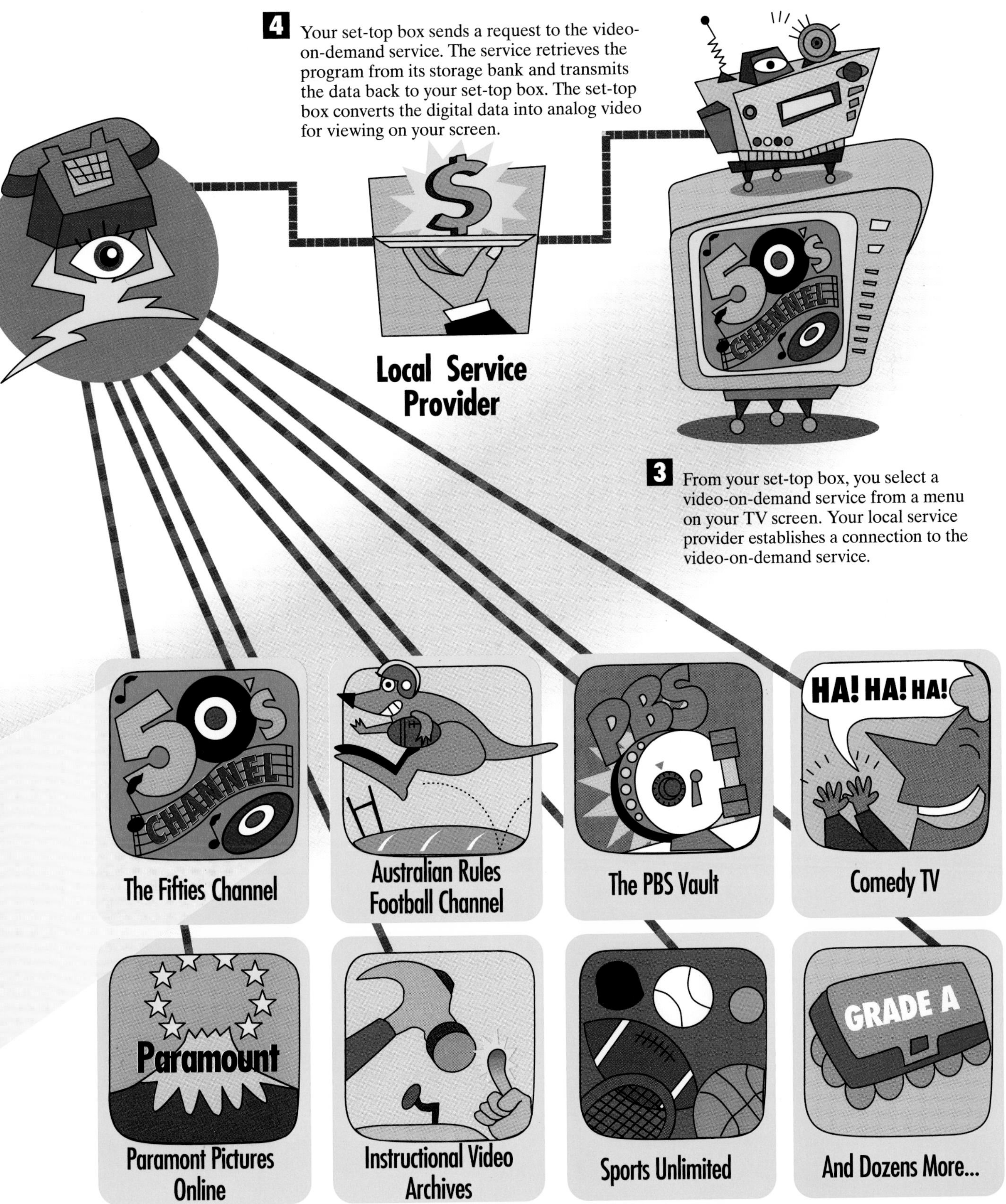
4 Your set-top box sends a request to the video-on-demand service. The service retrieves the program from its storage bank and transmits the data back to your set-top box. The set-top box converts the digital data into analog video for viewing on your screen.
Local Service Provider
3 From your set-top box, you select a video-on-demand service from a menu on your TV screen. Your local service provider establishes a connection to the video-on-demand service.
50's CHANNEL
The Fifties Channel
Australian Rules Football Channel
PBS
The PBS Vault
HA! HA! HA!
Comedy TV
Paramount
Paramont Pictures Online
Instructional Video Archives
Sports Unlimited
GRADE A
And Dozens More...

The Interactive TV Top Ten List

What will be the next killer app? Here's a list of the ten ideas that are vying for the honor and our opinion on whether or not they will succeed.

10 Interactive Game Shows No way. Truly interactive game shows have to be done live—and all these shows are taped. Besides, the logistics of 100,000 people trying to play "Wheel of Fortune" all at once just wouldn't work. It's likely that new games will be designed specifically for the interactive market, but this isn't the killer app.

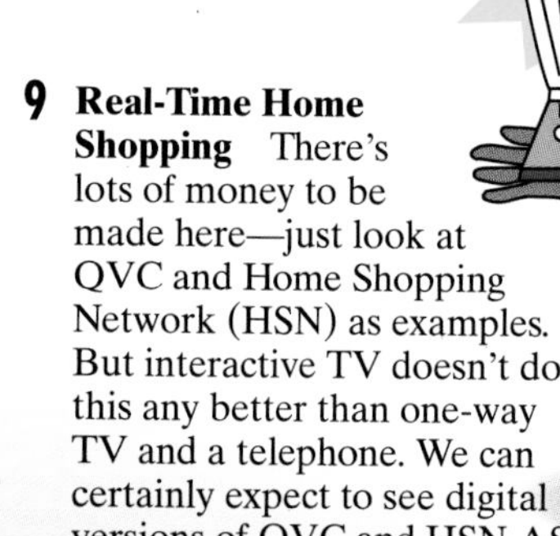

9 Real-Time Home Shopping There's lots of money to be made here—just look at QVC and Home Shopping Network (HSN) as examples. But interactive TV doesn't do this any better than one-way TV and a telephone. We can certainly expect to see digital versions of QVC and HSN ASAP.

8 Instant Opinion Polls Too esoteric. CNN and many local TV stations already do this with 800/900-number call-ins.

7 Home Banking Back when the PC explosion was just getting started, plenty of financial institutions lost money pursuing this idea. Money is too near and dear to people's hearts to be trusted to a computer. Besides, you can't get $20 bills out of a computer printer (not legally, anyway!).

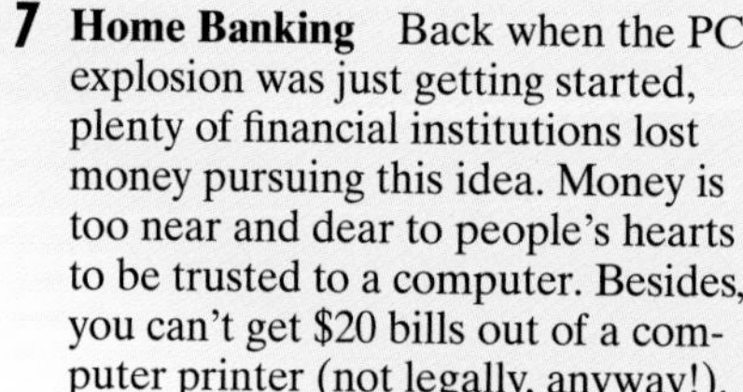

6 Telemedicine Now we're getting in to the "real" applications. This one is on the NII Agenda, and is likely to be a key part of any national health-care plan. Still, for any serious ailments, you'll want to see a real, live doctor—in person.

5 Two-Way TV We like this one. You plant a camera next to your TV, and call someone else who has a camera attached to their TV. It will be great for allowing grandparents to visit the kids without having to leave their condo in Florida. Downside: You'll need a lot of equipment and technical expertise to make this work.

4 Business Videoconferencing We like this one, too: You can "take a meeting" with your boss, peers, customers, whoever—all from your office conference room or home. You get the benefits of a face-to-face meeting without any of the expense or inconvenience.

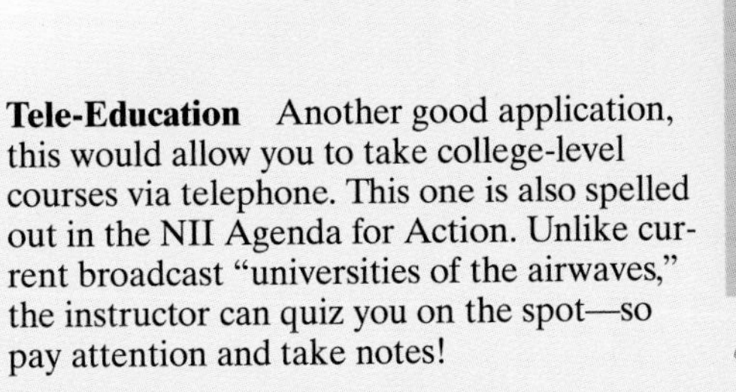

3 Tele-Education Another good application, this would allow you to take college-level courses via telephone. This one is also spelled out in the NII Agenda for Action. Unlike current broadcast "universities of the airwaves," the instructor can quiz you on the spot—so pay attention and take notes!

2 Interactive Video Games Here's every parent's nightmare—Johnny and Billy playing "Super Mario Bros. XVI" together—via long-distance. The idea here is that you can play video games with or against someone else, with the help of the highway. Sega has already demonstrated an interactive gaming system, and more are sure to follow.

1 Interactive Advertising This could be the killer app. Imagine a vast video catalog of goods and services—free of connect charges. Shopping for a new car? Check the Pontiac channel, where you can take a video test drive, read product specifications, and check out the available colors—without a salesperson. Want to see the latest New York fashions? Dial up Fashion TV, where you can select from a menu of designers. Shopping for a new word processor? Dial up the software channel, and download a demo version of the latest version of your favorite WP program. If you like it, you can download the full version of the program and charge it to your credit card.

Where Does the PC Fit In?

AFTER TEN YEARS of effort and billions of dollars in investment, the market for PCs in the home is finally opening up—just in time to connect home PCs to the digital highway. Multimedia, the same technology that's being used to sell home computer systems, may also prove to be the biggest selling point for the digital highway. In fact, multimedia applications and hardware are the fastest growing segment in the computer marketplace.

Multimedia technology combines graphics, sound, and full-motion video. It's being used to create everything from electronic encyclopedias to realistic computer games. Because graphics, sound, and video require large amounts of storage space, the *CD-ROM* (compact disc read-only memory) has become the distribution medium of choice for multimedia applications. CD-ROMs look just like audio CDs and both can be produced using the same equipment. Of course, you need a CD-ROM drive connected to your computer to take advantage of this technology.

After several years of false starts, sales of CD-ROM drives and multimedia software are soaring. Multimedia technology has evolved into the killer app that has finally allowed the computer manufacturers to penetrate the elusive (and potentially huge) home market for PCs. Users who were left cold by the text-based, command-driven interface of early PCs are lining up to buy the new generation of graphically interfaced, multimedia-ready home PCs. Of course, a major decrease in PC prices hasn't hurt, either.

Most PC vendors now offer at least one "home office" system, which usually includes a CD-ROM drive, sound board, and several multimedia software titles. In the Macintosh universe, Apple offers several machines with built-in CD-ROM drives, and all Macs are equipped with quality sound reproduction hardware.

Microsoft and Apple both offer integrated multimedia software, including support for full-motion video. In a rare show of compatibility, both companies support Apple's QuickTime video technology. This allows CD-ROM software developers to easily offer their wares for both the Macintosh and PC platforms.

Many industry watchers (ourselves included) see multimedia as a stepping stone on the way to much bigger and better things—in this case, to the digital highway. While CD-ROM drives have improved dramatically over the past few years, the CD-ROM format itself has several limitations.

First, much of the material available on CD-ROM becomes outdated quickly, meaning that you'll need to buy updates for your favorite CDs. Second, CD-ROMs can hold 580MB of data. While this is a staggering amount of text, it's not all that much data when you're talking about full-motion video. Microsoft's Encarta encyclopedia, for example, contains thousands of still pictures, but only a precious few (22) full-motion video clips. There's just not enough room on a CD-ROM to provide a video clip for every subject. Still, it's the video clips that make multimedia happen. The few clips scattered throughout Encarta are the chocolate chips that make the rest of the cookie so tempting.

But the biggest problem with CD-ROMs isn't a technical one. Users simply get tired of seeing the same thing over and over. Multimedia CD-ROMs aren't cheap—a typical CD-ROM encyclopedia lists for $149—so running out to the local software store for something new can be expensive.

But suppose multimedia junkies could just dial into, for example, Encarta Online, where they could browse through an encyclopedia that *does* have video clips for every subject. The underlying technology is the same—it's just the distribution method that's different. The difference is analogous to owning a few books (that you read over and over), or having access to a complete library.

As we'll see in the next chapter, several subscription information services (CompuServe, Prodigy, and America Online, to name a few) are poised and ready to deliver on-line multimedia information to your desktop PC. Today's modem technology, with its low bandwidth, limits the amount and type of data that these services can deliver today. You can bet that these services will be among the first to make the move to the digital highway.

How Multimedia Works

A CD-ROM looks just like an audio CD. But in addition to digital audio, a CD-ROM can store video, text, and computer software.

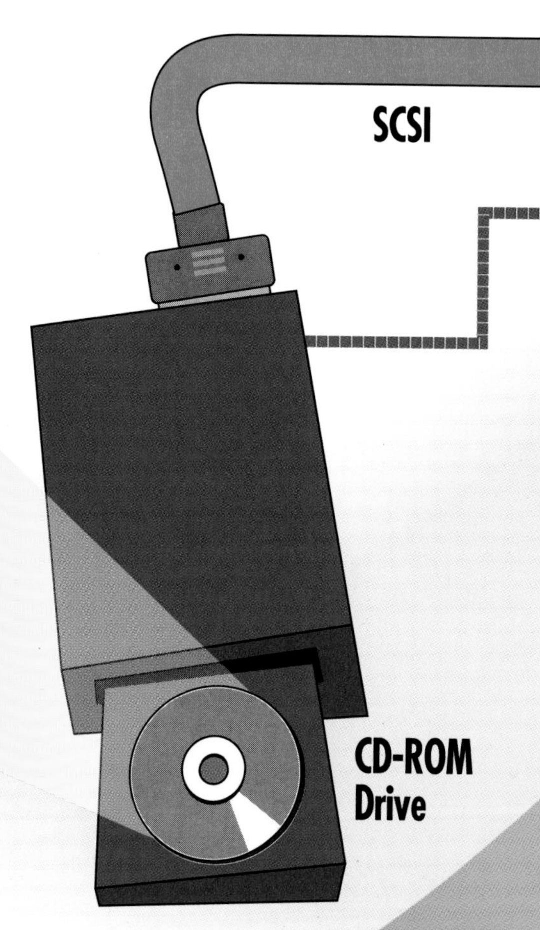

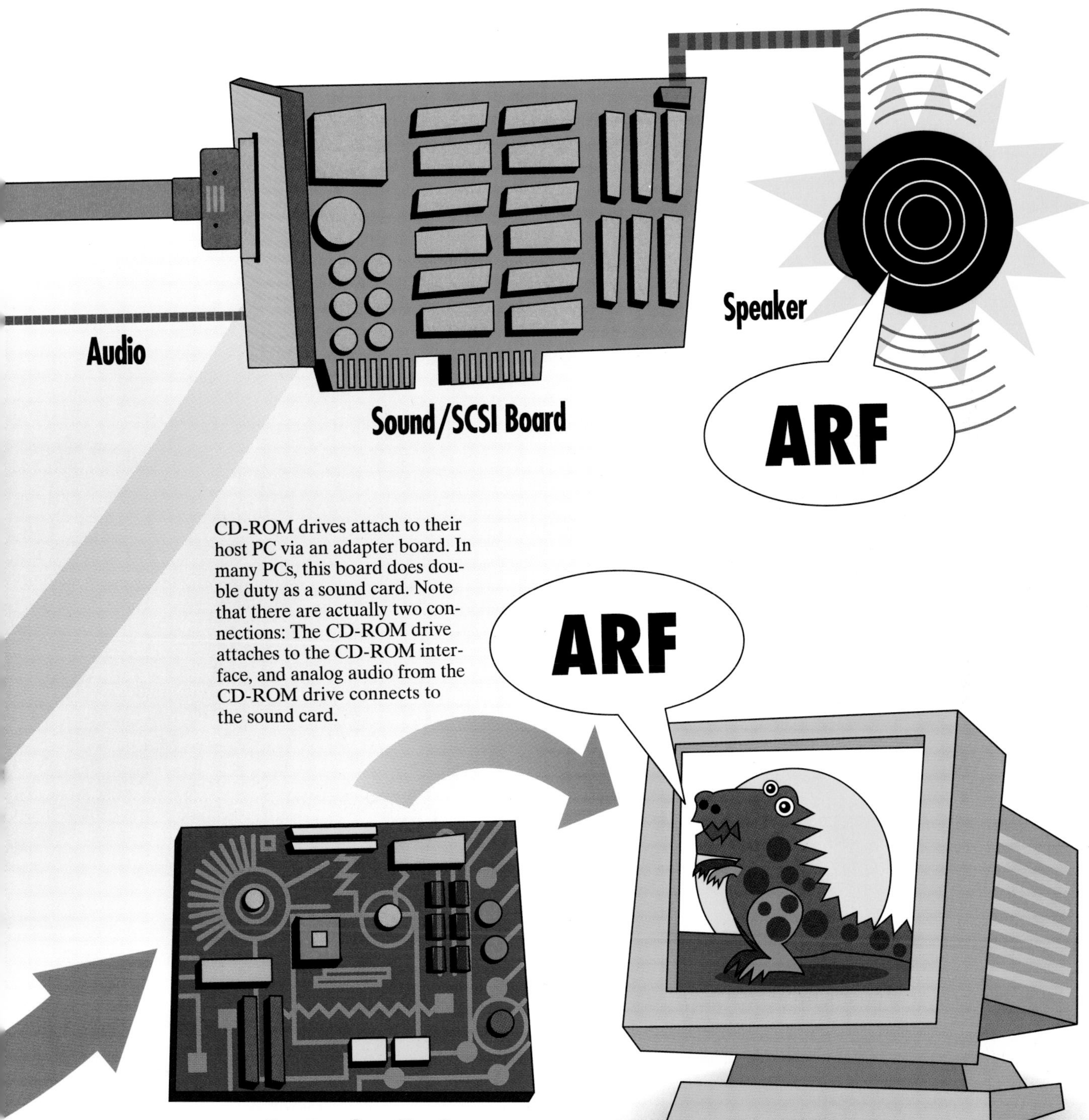

CD-ROM drives attach to their host PC via an adapter board. In many PCs, this board does double duty as a sound card. Note that there are actually two connections: The CD-ROM drive attaches to the CD-ROM interface, and analog audio from the CD-ROM drive connects to the sound card.

The multimedia software running on the computer brings all the elements together. The software controls the CD-ROM drive, reading and storing data from the disk. Much of this data is digital pictures, which are usually stored in a compressed format to save space. The software must decompress the video and pass the resulting image along to the PC's video display.

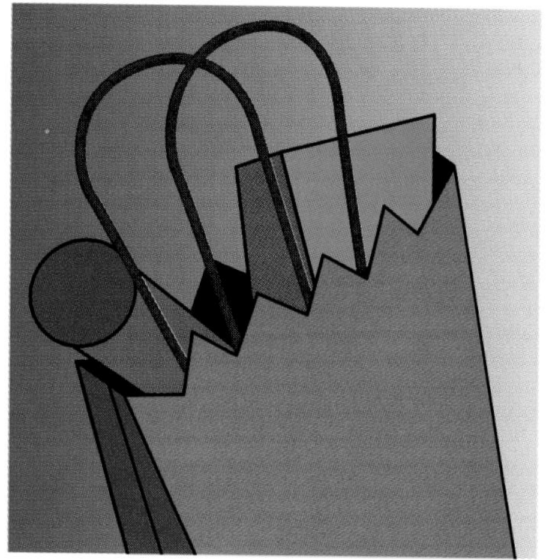

On-Line Services: Superstores on the Superhighway

WE'VE ALL SEEN this happen: A new highway is built in the middle of nowhere. Before long, the highway is lined with gas stations, motels, and shopping malls. After a few years, the highway is jammed with shoppers and commuters, and the road needs to be widened. A similar thing has happened with on-line information services. In many ways, on-line information services are the pioneers of the digital highway. They've been here since the digital highway was a slow, dusty back road, and they're jockeying to become your favorite off-ramp once the high-bandwidth digital highway is complete.

From very humble beginnings in the late 1970s, on-line services have grown into a major industry. Worldwide membership in on-line information services has grown from a few thousand users in the late 1970s to over 5 million in 1993. The digital roadways into the information services are bottlenecked due to today's relatively low-speed modem technology. There are occasional traffic jams, and even when the roadway is clear, the traffic moves slowly.

On-line services provide a wide range of services to millions of users each day. It's difficult to categorize these services because so many people use them in so many different ways. Basically, they are on-line information shopping malls—a place where you can get news, sports, stock quotes, research materials, and software updates. You can also play games, exchange electronic mail (e-mail), order flowers and plane tickets, or join a discussion group. Some services charge a monthly flat fee, while others charge by the hour.

It's interesting to note who the players are in the information service business. There's big money to be made here, and the industry has attracted a strange mix of contenders. Prodigy is a joint venture of Sears and IBM. GEnie belongs to General Electric Corporation. CompuServe is owned by H&R Block, the income-tax preparation giants, and America Online's largest shareholder is Paul Allen, co-founder of Microsoft. Delphi was recently purchased by newspaper mogul Rupert Murdoch.

Currently, the only way users can access these services is through a personal computer equipped with a modem—the digital equivalent of a two-lane road. Thanks to the popularity of graphical user interfaces (GUIs) like Apple's Macintosh and Microsoft's Windows, access to the information services is easier than ever. CompuServe, Prodigy, GEnie, and America Online all provide "point and click" interface software that allows users to navigate through the services by pointing and clicking with a tracking device such as a mouse.

Being text-based isn't necessarily a bad thing, and there are many useful services available on-line. In fact, the majority of information services are text-based—despite the attractive graphical interface—because moving pictures and sound require more bandwidth than modems can provide. So, for example, if you want to see the latest news from the Associated Press on CompuServe, you dial up CompuServe with your computer and modem, click on AP News from a menu of services, and read the news on your screen—much like you'd read a newspaper.

CompuServe and Prodigy have begun to offer limited graphics as part of their basic service, thanks to faster modems. For example, a news story on Prodigy's headline page may have a color still picture attached to it. Click on the See Picture button at the bottom of the screen, and the picture appears on your screen. It's not full-motion color video with stereo sound, but it's a start.

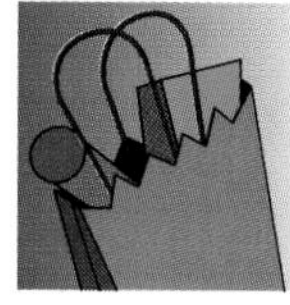

We can expect a whole new range of services once direct digital access—with much higher bandwidth—to these services becomes possible. For example, instead of reading today's news headlines as text, you'll be able to pick from a group of video clips and so create your own news program. When you dial up CompuServe to order flowers, you'll be able to see a full-color picture of each selection. When you make an airline reservation, you'll be able to see an overhead view of the available seats. Click your mouse on the seat you want, and it'll be reserved for you.

An On-Line Information Service

An on-line information service resembles a shopping mall. Merchandise (in this case, information) arrives by the truckload on high-speed T1 and T3 circuits. The information is stored in the appropriate department so that customers can find it.

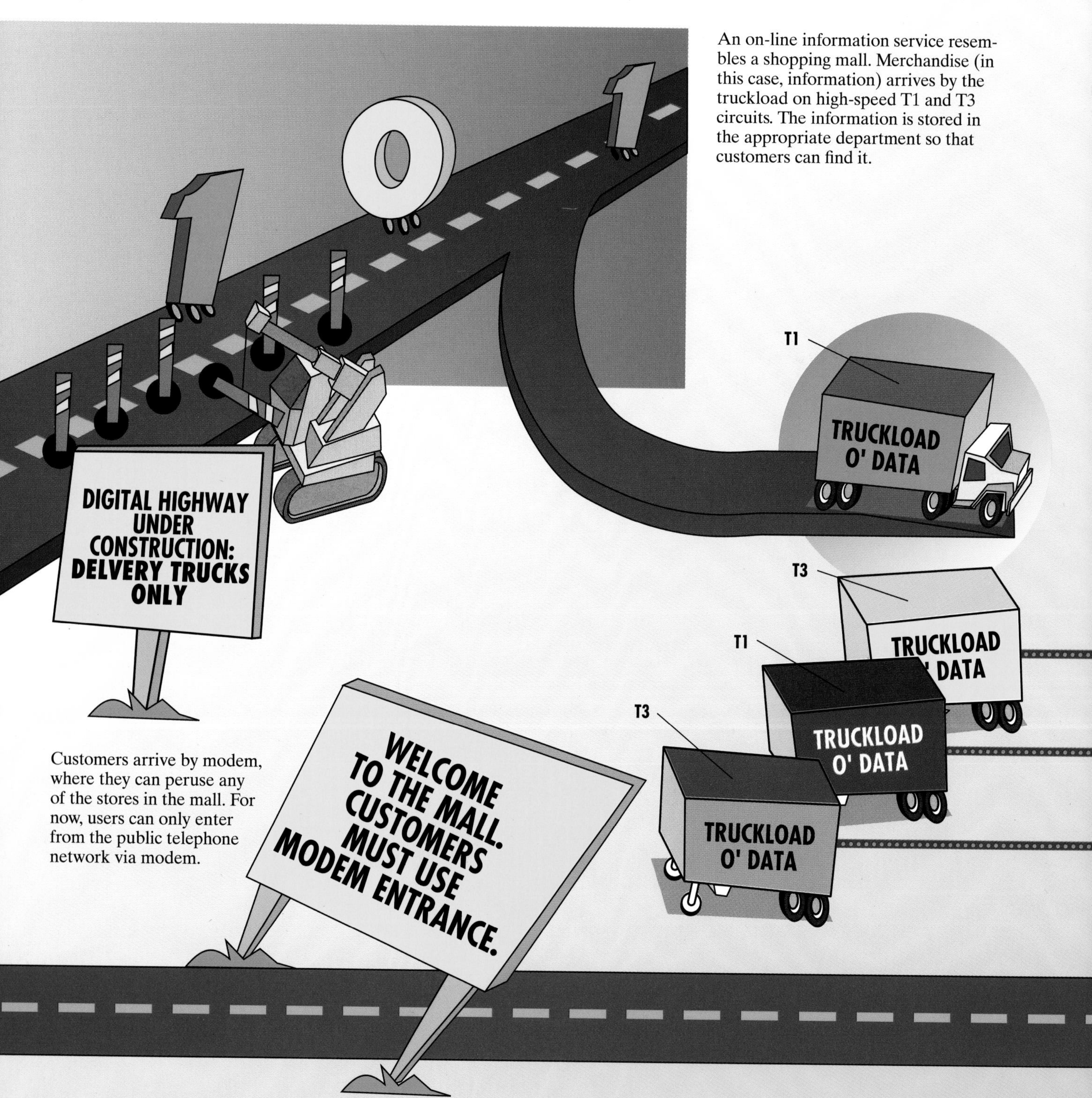

Customers arrive by modem, where they can peruse any of the stores in the mall. For now, users can only enter from the public telephone network via modem.

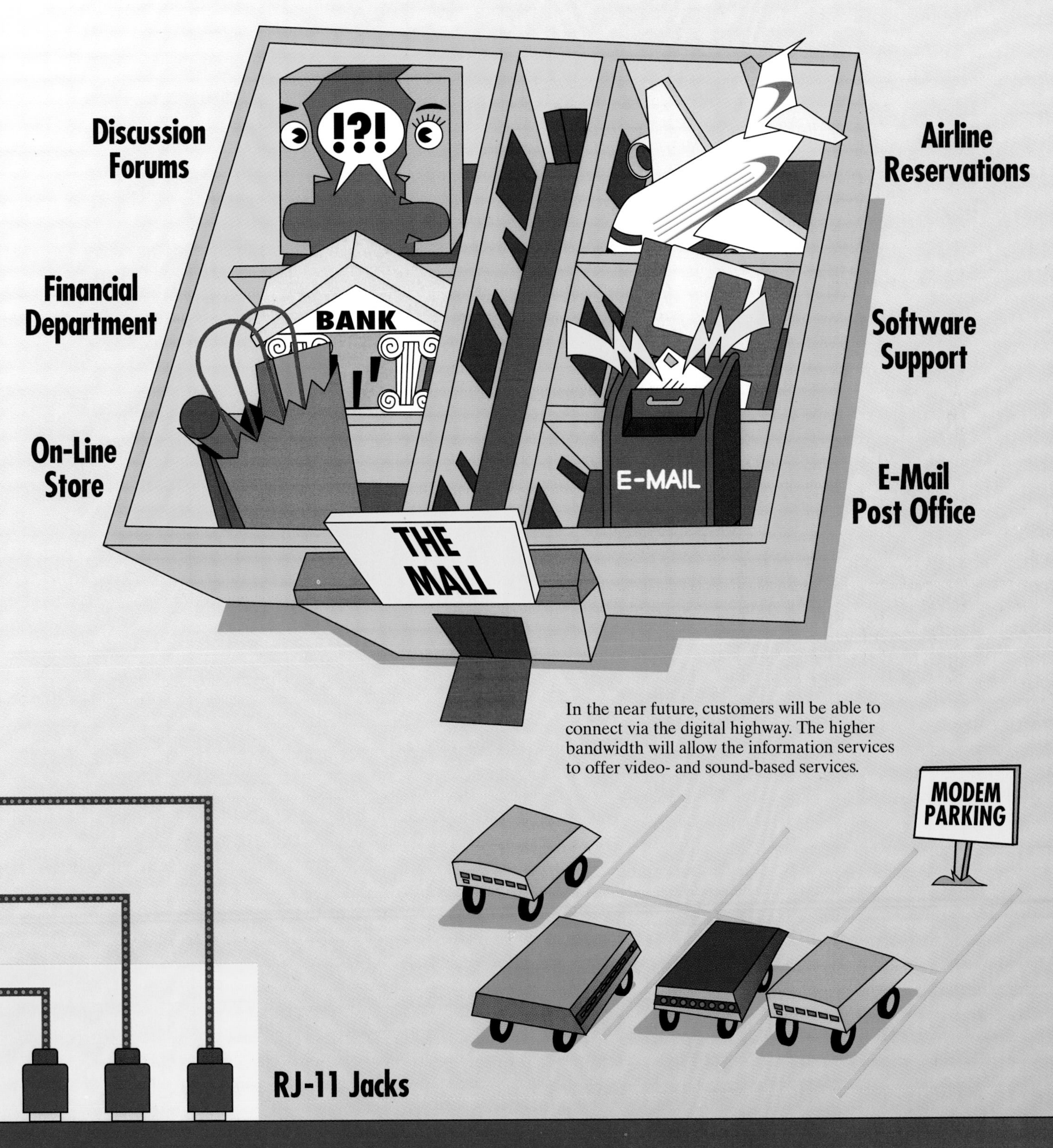

In the near future, customers will be able to connect via the digital highway. The higher bandwidth will allow the information services to offer video- and sound-based services.

The Internet

IF THERE IS a working prototype for the digital highway, that prototype is the Internet. The Internet is an international network of computer networks. Over 25 million people worldwide have access to the Internet, and it is estimated that an additional 30,000 new people come on-line each day.

What exactly is the Internet? This is a tough question to answer. It's sort of an electronic amoeba, connecting computers all over the world. Through the magic of the Internet, users can download files, join discussion groups, exchange electronic mail (e-mail), and connect to computers all over the world. The amazing part is that access to the Internet is very inexpensive, and often free!

The Internet actually began in the 1960s as the Advanced Research Projects Agency Network (ARPANET), which was funded by the U.S. Department of Defense. The basic idea behind ARPANET was to allow scientists and researchers easy access to each other's information. In the 1980s the National Science Foundation (NSF) officially created the Internet, replacing the original ARPANET with a more modern, higher-speed network. The NSF's original goal for the Internet was to provide access to four government-owned (and horribly expensive) supercomputers. Although it was originally intended as a research and educational network, the Internet has grown to include a large number of businesses and commercial services as well.

The Internet consists of thousands of computers worldwide. Using a facility called Telnet, any individual user on the Internet can connect to any computer on the Internet. A computer that provides services to other users is called a host computer. Once connected to a host, a user can run programs on the host as if he or she were sitting at a terminal directly connected to the host system. Telnet is a very powerful tool, and it is one of the main communication tools used on the Internet. Telnet hosts may provide anything from multiplayer computer games, to access to specialized information on AIDS research.

The File Transfer Protocol (FTP) is another useful Internet function. Internet users can take advantage of FTP to copy files from a host system to their own computer. Earlier in this book, we quoted excerpts from the NII Agenda for Action. We received our copy of that document via FTP directly from the federal government. There are millions of files available on the Internet, and any user has access to them. In fact, there are so many hosts containing so many files that some hosts are dedicated to the task of helping users sift through that information. Special hosts called *Archie servers* keep track of all the files that are publicly posted on the Internet. If you want to locate files on a specific topic, you can use an Archie server to help you find those files.

Virtually all hosts on the Internet can exchange e-mail. This allows any user to send mail to any other user on the Internet. In most cases, e-mail is free of charge. In the past few years, virtually all of the on-line information services like CompuServe and Prodigy have connected their mail systems to the Internet. This allows users on any of the major on-line services to exchange mail with any user on any other service.

In addition to e-mail, the Internet is host to a global conferencing system called Usenet. Usenet is essentially an open forum conducted via e-mail. There are thousands of Usenet discussion topics, and new topics are added almost daily. Some discussions are highly esoteric in nature. For example, the Internet address rec.org.sca is devoted to the Society for Creative Anachronism. On the other hand, many discussions are of broader interest. The addresses comp.sys.ibm and comp.sys.mac, for instance, contain a wealth of useful information for computer users. For many people, Usenet is the Internet's killer app.

The Internet was designed to link computers, and it performs that task very well. Today's Internet is the result of millions of hours of programming work, much of it done by programmers working for free. The Internet has fostered dozens of breakthroughs in communications technology, and we can expect to see much of that technology transplanted to the digital highway project.

The Internet

There are thousands of host computers on the Internet. Some are directly attached to the backbone, but most connect via leased telephone lines. In this example, a user in Tampa is connecting to a host computer in Seattle.

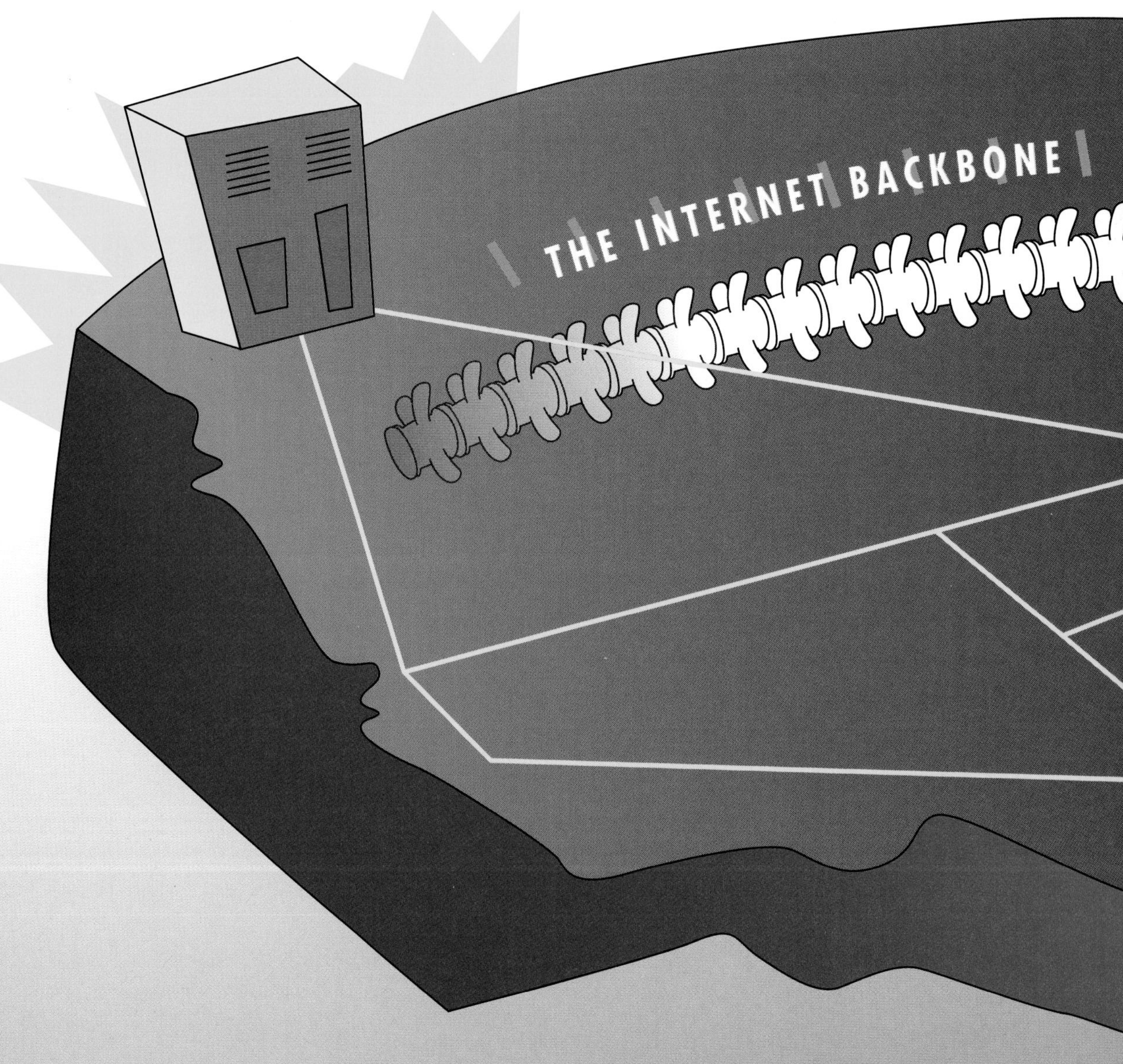

The major connecting members of the Internet are called the backbone network. The backbone is a long-distance, high-speed digital link funded by the National Science Foundation.

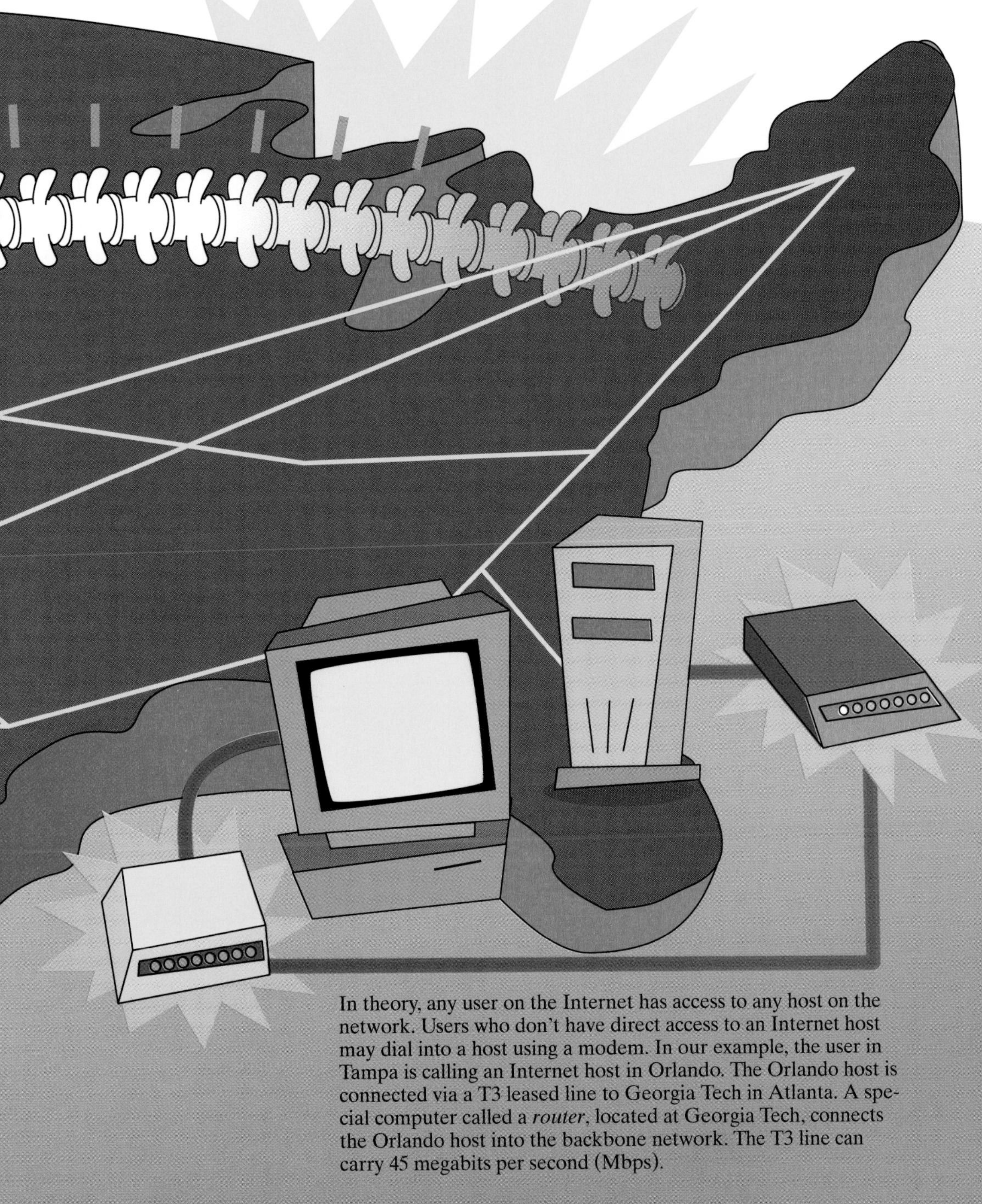

In theory, any user on the Internet has access to any host on the network. Users who don't have direct access to an Internet host may dial into a host using a modem. In our example, the user in Tampa is calling an Internet host in Orlando. The Orlando host is connected via a T3 leased line to Georgia Tech in Atlanta. A special computer called a *router*, located at Georgia Tech, connects the Orlando host into the backbone network. The T3 line can carry 45 megabits per second (Mbps).

The Virtual Internet

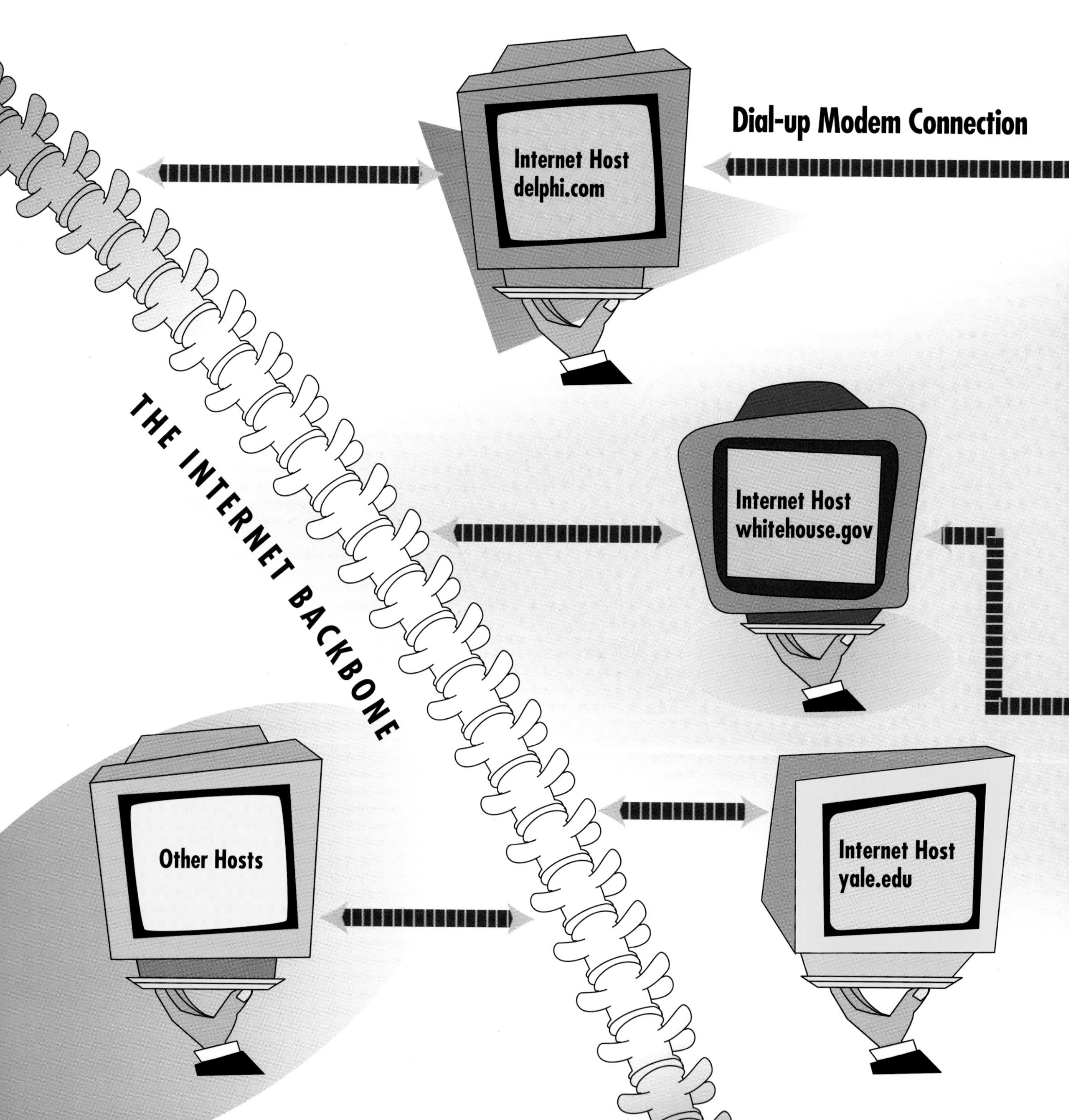

Each user on the Internet has a unique user name. For example, Les's Delphi user name is lfreed. When he connects to the Internet through Delphi, he becomes lfreed@delphi.com. Note that user names are usually all lowercase.

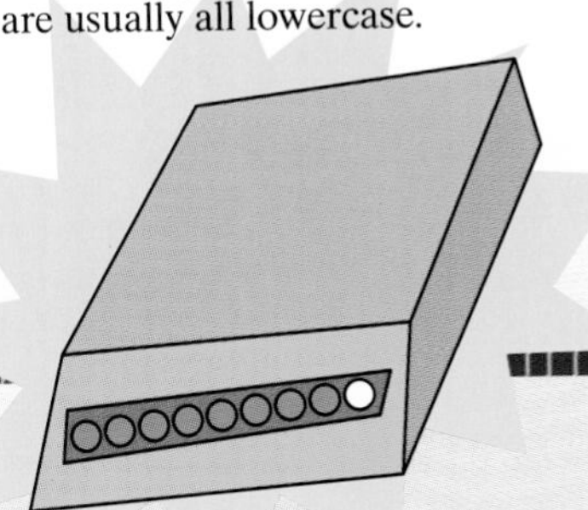

The thousands of computers on the Internet appear to the users as an almost seamless network of hosts. All you need to know to use a host is its name, and all you need to know to send e-mail to someone is that person's user name. No matter where you are or how you connect to the Internet, all the hosts are always available—just as if they were all directly connected to your host.

Each host computer on the Internet has a unique name. In addition to the name, each host has a three-letter suffix to indicate the nature of the organization operating the host. For example, commercial services use the suffix .com, and government agencies use .gov. Other suffixes you'll see are .mil (military), .edu (educational institutions), .org (organizations), and .net (network administrators).

Do-It-Yourself Publishing

THE FOUNDING FATHERS did it. So did Stewart Brand, Rush Limbaugh, and a host of Jamaican reggae bands. *Wired* magazine does it all the time.

What is "it?" Publishing their own material. Unable or unwilling to find a traditional outlet for their creations, they created their own outlets.

New technologies like computerized music composition, desktop publishing, and desktop video have made it easier than ever to produce professional-quality music, print, and video pieces. Anyone with a PC and a little computer expertise can create anything from a poetry newsletter to a rock video at relatively low cost. Distributing those works to a broad audience is the hard part. Until now, budding novelists, film producers, poets, musicians, and other creative artists have had to sell their products to a publisher, record company, TV network, or other media distribution organization.

In our media-conscious society, we often know as much about the publisher of a work as we do about the work itself. Somewhere in our mental filing cabinets, we know that Ziff-Davis publishes computer books and magazines, that Doubleday is big in novels, and that Time-Life produces news magazines and coffee-table books. So what does an author/writer/musician/poet do when his or her work doesn't fit any one publisher's marketing plans? In most cases, nothing. But all that is about to change.

Numerous authors, musicians, and entrepreneurs have turned to self-publishing when their plans, product, or politics didn't mesh with the existing publishing outlets. One of the most famous examples is the highly successful *Whole Earth Catalog*. Originally conceived by Stewart Brand as a sourcebook for the '60s counterculture, *Whole Earth* spawned an industry of its own, including an on-line service.

At the other end of the political spectrum, commentator Rush Limbaugh syndicates his own radio and TV shows over his own "Excellence in Broadcasting" network. Try as we may, we can't imagine Rush on CBS or NBC; going it alone has brought him fame and, no doubt, considerable fortune.

So what does all this have to do with the digital highway? Everything. The arts are entering the digital age. On the Internet, for example, you'll find discussions and exchanges of poetry, photography, music, drama, video production, and fiction—among thousands of other topics. Similarly, CompuServe's discussion forums contain articles on these same topics, along with downloadable copies of poems, photos, digital movies, and musical works. These electronic forums give amateur artists the chance to bring their works to the public. The audience is small—at least for right now—but very focused.

The self-publishing trend hasn't gone unnoticed by the conventional media outlets. In November 1993, Electronic Cafe International (ECI) opened the first of its 60 "coffeehouses." A sort of rest stop on the digital highway, the Electronic Cafe links poets, musicians, and performers in 60 cities, using big-screen television, CD-quality digital audio, and interconnected electronic musical instruments. The ECI network uses a digital telephone service called ISDN (more on ISDN in Chapter 15) to connect any cafe to any of the others. ISDN service is widely available in most major cities, so adding new cafes won't be a technological hurdle. The ECI concept is an interesting idea, but more interesting is that the New York cafe is owned by Viacom International (the company that owns the MTV, VH-1, Showtime, and Nickelodeon cable networks). Viacom has a well-deserved reputation for spotting new trends, and ECI could well be the start of a worldwide network of artists, musicians, poets, and performers.

The Digital Cafe

Our digital cafe features a live concert by a jazz pianist in Los Angeles and a classical violinist in New York. Big-screen TVs in each cafe provide a view of the other cafe, and microphones pick up the sound at each location.

The analog video and sound are fed into a PC at each location. The PCs are equipped with digital-to-analog (D/A) and analog-to-digital (A/D) converter cards that convert the camera's picture and microphone's audio into digital form for transmission over the ISDN network. The PCs also convert incoming digital data back into analog video and sound for display on the big-screen TV. In addition, the PCs compress data, squeezing a full-motion picture and hi-fi sound into a single ISDN connection.

Audiences in both locations can see the performance. Additional cameras focused on the audiences allow them to see each other.

A Day in the Life

WHAT WILL THE digital future be like? We've always wanted to write a sci-fi novel, but the folks at Ziff-Davis Press keep us too busy writing computer books. This chapter could have been science fiction just a few years ago; today, it's a glimpse into the near future.

8:00 You are awakened by a specially coded signal from your bedside telephone. The beep-beep-beep pattern of the phone, which you programmed the night before, reminds you that you have an important business meeting later this morning. Just to be sure you remember correctly, you pick up the phone and hear a reminder message to yourself in your own voice: "Videoconference with Global Gizmos at ten o'clock." You notice that it is pouring rain outside.

8:10 You get up and have a cup of coffee while you peruse the morning's news. Instead of a rain-soaked newspaper or a commercial-filled TV news broadcast, you read a customized newspaper on your PC, downloaded from the CBS NewsNet server ten minutes before you awoke. The newspaper contains the developments of the night before, omitting articles that you've already seen. On the sports menu, you notice that your favorite baseball team won a 13-inning thriller of a game. You click on the film icon at the bottom of the article, and a 90-second color video game summary appears, showing all the key plays of the game.

8:30 It's time to go to work, so you hop in the car and pull out of the driveway. Just as you're about to turn onto the expressway, your cellular phone rings, and a digitized voice warns you that the expressway is backed up due to a major accident five minutes ago. You pass up the expressway on-ramp and proceed a few miles out of your way, following the route provided by the traffic monitor service. As you pass over the expressway, all you can see below is miles of taillights.

9:00 You're at the office on time. You spend a few minutes reading your mail (much of which contains voice and video clips from your fellow workers), and at 9:50, you start the videoconferencing program on your PC.

10:00 The conference begins, connecting you with several coworkers around the country. Each of your PCs has a tiny camera mounted on its monitor, so each participant's face appears in a window on the screen.

12:00 Lunchtime. You're finished at the office, and you decide to spend the rest of the day working at home. Since it's midday, there's virtually no traffic on the expressway, and you get home quickly. You drive through the tollbooth without even stopping; your car has a bar-code toll decal that's read automatically as you drive through.

1:00 You spend the afternoon working on a proposal at home on your PC. You dial up the office and transmit a copy of your proposal to your boss via electronic mail.

5:00 Quitting time. You dial up CompuServe with your PC and check into the fly-fishing forum. Another member has posted a how-to video, showing how to tie a hot new fly that's tearing up the redfish along the Gulf coast. You view the video, then file a copy away on your PC's hard disk.

6:00 The kids are hungry, and you don't feel like cooking, so you dial up the Digital Deli take-out service. You choose a main dish from your favorite Chinese restaurant, and a dessert from a French pastry shop. Thirty minutes later, the driver appears at your door with your order. You don't have to fumble for cash, since you charged the meal (and the driver's tip) to your electronic funds-transfer account.

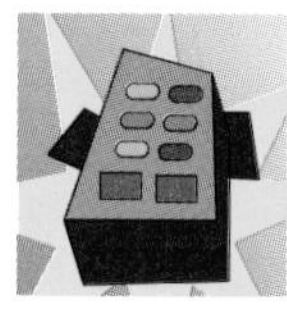

7:00 Time to catch up on the day's news. You cruise through the news offerings on your big-screen TV, using the set-top box remote control to scan the offerings. You settle on CNN's menu-driven news feed, which allows you to pick the stories you want to see.

8:00 The kids want to see *Wayne's World III*, so you decide to let them order the movie on interactive cable. You retire to the den and read a good, old-fashioned paper book published a few years ago. It's called *Building the Information Highway*. You amuse yourself by comparing the authors' forecasts to your current reality.

Your Digital Day

How will the digital highway technology affect our daily lives? We offer this look at the typical day in the life of a typical digital highway user. Note that many of the technologies shown here exist today.

8:10 am

SPORTS FINALS

8:30 am

TRAFFIC JAM AHEAD!

9:00 am

10:00 am

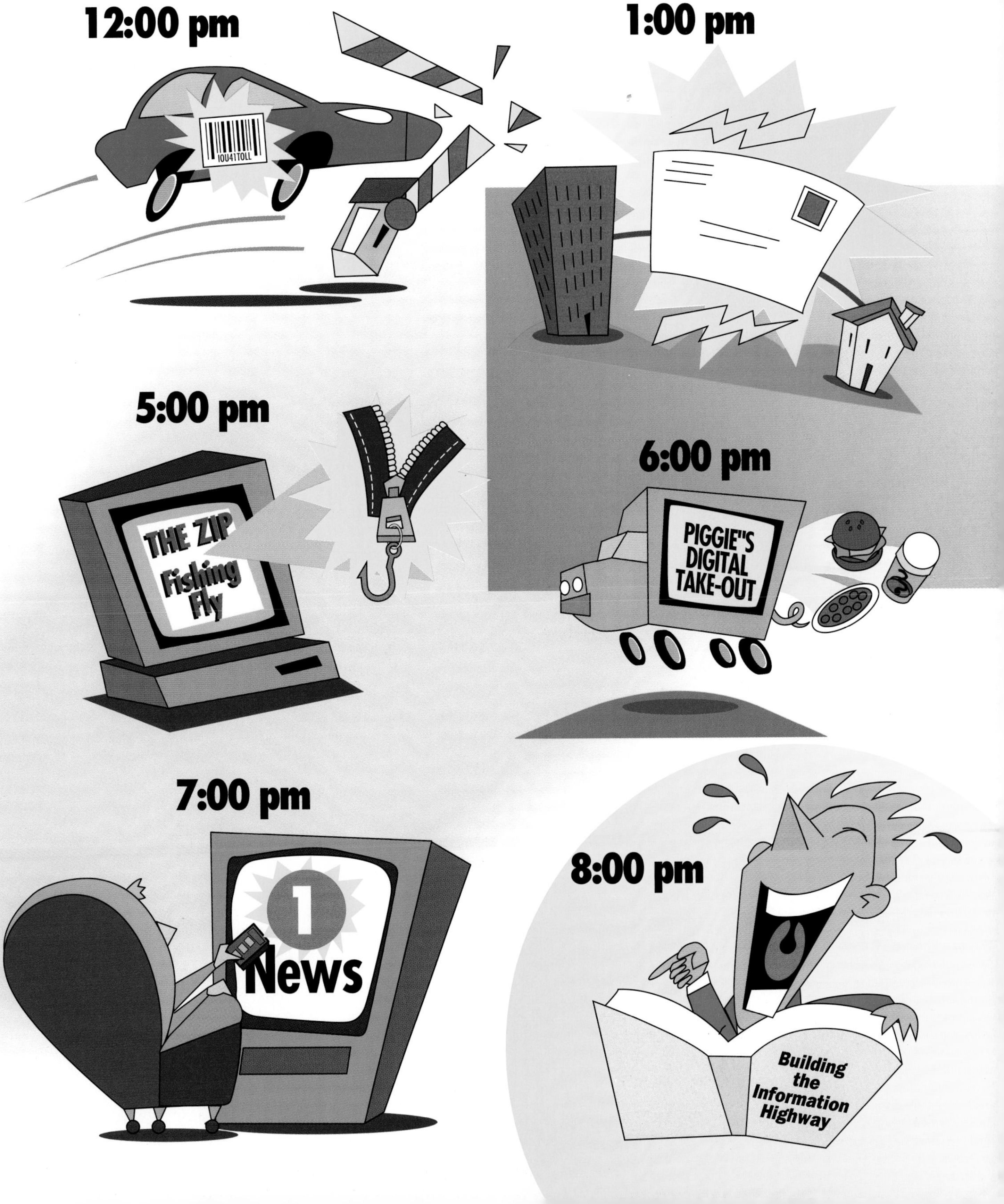

12:00 pm

1:00 pm

5:00 pm

6:00 pm

7:00 pm

8:00 pm

Who's Watching Whom?

IF YOU'VE EVER seen the TV spy show "Mission: Impossible," or any old detective movies, you know how ridiculously easy it is to tap a telephone. Anyone with access to your telephone wires can tap in and listen to or record your telephone conversations.

Although wiretapping is illegal (unless done by a police agency with a court's permission), illegal wiretapping happens all the time. Unauthorized access to credit card information, banking records, stock transactions, and other sensitive data can provide criminals with an electronic gold mine of fraud opportunities.

As we move to an all-digital communication system, we have the opportunity to correct some of the shortcomings of the older, analog system. Because analog telephone lines carry analog audio signals, listening in doesn't require any special equipment—a telephone with the mouthpiece switched off is a favorite tapper's tool.

Digital signals are more difficult to decode than analog signals, but if a wiretapper knows what type of signal to expect on the wire, digital lines are about as easy to tap as a regular telephone. Because digital signals are simply a series of electrical ones and zeros, it is also relatively simple to scramble, or *encrypt*, digital data. Encrypted data appears to an interloper as a meaningless jumble.

There are several standard encryption schemes in use today. One of the most widely used is called *Data Encryption Standard* (DES). DES is the official encryption technique used by the federal government. DES uses a 64-bit binary number as an electronic "key." The data to be sent is mathematically scrambled with the key, effectively producing an electronic "lock" with 72 quadrillion possible combinations. As secure as this sounds, there are two major problems with DES.

First, as computers become more powerful, it becomes easier to write a program that can break the DES code. Still, DES is secure enough for most business and personal uses, and should remain so for at least another ten years. Second, both the sender and receiver must know the key in order to unlock the encrypted data. This means that the sender must send a copy of the key to the recipient, thereby risking a possible security breach.

Public Key Encryption—also known as RSA encryption because of its inventors (Rivest, Shamir, and Adleman)—is another widely used encryption technique. RSA encryption uses a two-part key. Under the RSA scheme, data is encrypted using the recipient's public key. Once encrypted, the data can only be encrypted with the recipient's private key. The private key is known only to the recipient, but the public key may be freely distributed without compromising security.

Because RSA encryption requires a great deal of computing horsepower, it is currently impractical for use with lengthy messages. RSA is most often used to create a *digital envelope*. The envelope contains an RSA-encrypted DES key, which can then be used to decode a DES-encrypted method. Thus, because the public key can be freely passed around without compromising security, RSA solves the problem of passing a key along with a DES-encoded message.

The federal government is concerned about the widespread availability of data encryption technology. The FBI and other investigative agencies have relied on wiretaps for years, and now they fear that one of their most important tools may become useless. Furthermore, the widespread use of data encryption gives a new tool to the bad guys.

Enter Clipper. *Clipper* is a government-sponsored data encryption method, similar to RSA in that it uses a public key and a private key. The government wants Clipper to be the only data encryption plan approved for use on the digital highway. If the Clipper plan is adopted, all other data encryption techniques will be outlawed.

The Clipper plan is based on the Clipper chip—a special-purpose chip designed specifically for data encryption. Because Clipper encryption is done in hardware, it is much faster than software-based encryption. But there's a major catch.

Under the government's plan, all Clipper users would be required to register their private keys with an escrow agent. If the FBI or another law enforcement agency feels that there is sufficient evidence of wrongdoing, the government can get a court order to gain access to the suspect's private key.

The Clipper plan has raised a major ruckus among a wide cross-section of the computing community. Civil libertarians (for instance, members of the Electronic Freedom Foundation) say the Clipper plan gives the government too much leeway in deciding whose data to monitor. Technologists claim that the Clipper encryption scheme is technically weak and will be outdated in a few years. Other opponents point out that even if the Clipper plan is adopted, the bad guys will simply use another, non-government-approved encryption scheme.

An Encrypted Telephone Conversation

1 As the woman on the left speaks, the sound waves of her voice are converted into digital data. The data passes through an encryption circuit, which scrambles the data, using the receiver's public key.

3 At the other end, a decryption circuit uses the receiver's private key to restore the data to its original form. The data passes through a digital-to-analog converter and is converted back into sound waves.

2 The encrypted data appears to a potential wiretapper as a meaningless stream of random data.

3 BUILDING A DIGITAL WORLD

CONTENTS

IF YOU'RE READING this book, you're probably the type of person who likes to stay abreast of the latest in technology. You probably have a television, a stereo, a VCR, and a telephone. You probably think that they're the latest, greatest, highest-tech toys available, and they are—sort of.

It may surprise you to learn that our existing electronic communications media—the telephone, radio, and television—haven't changed much since their creation. Alexander Graham Bell would recognize much of today's telephone system, and Guglielmo Marconi would have no trouble understanding how today's radio works. Philo T. Farnsworth and Vladimir Zworykin, the fathers of television, would understand exactly how today's television works. Granted, there have been ongoing technical improvements and innovations since these inventions first appeared. None of these historical figures foresaw the advent of satellites, videotape, or cable TV. TV has progressed from monochrome to color, and FM radio has progressed from monaural to stereo. Thanks to some clever engineering, these improvements were backward-compatible with their predecessors. You can still watch a color broadcast on a black-and-white TV, and you can listen to stereo FM broadcasts on a monaural radio.

In addition, radio, TV, and the telephone still use analog signal technology—a technology that dates back to Bell's first telephone in 1876. We're stuck in a technological stone age because of the success of these three key inventions. There are over 100 million telephones, 100 million television sets, and countless AM and FM radios in the United States. Any radically new technology—like an all-digital communications network—will eventually make existing equipment obsolete.

Of course, today's radio, TV, and telephone networks aren't going to disappear overnight. Even low-tech information tools such as magazines and newspapers will likely be with us for a long time. But bear in mind the surprising speed with which the compact disk replaced the venerable LP record. Once record buyers heard their first high-quality CD, they rushed to the stores in droves, buying CDs by the millions.

Digital compact discs are a major improvement over analog vinyl LP records. They don't wear out, don't scratch as easily, and provide a level of sound quality that simply wasn't attainable with vinyl. If you thought audio CDs were a big improvement, wait until you see digital television. Digital video is sharper and clearer, with resolution and shadow detail previously obtainable only with 35mm film. Digital TV will bring theater-quality pictures and CD-quality sound to your living room. As we'll see in Part 3 of this book, much of the technology used to build the digital highway will come from the computer industry. Existing computer networking technologies will be adapted and expanded to accomodate digital video and sound. The resulting convergence of television, computer networking, and electronic communication technologies will likely be with us for many years to come.

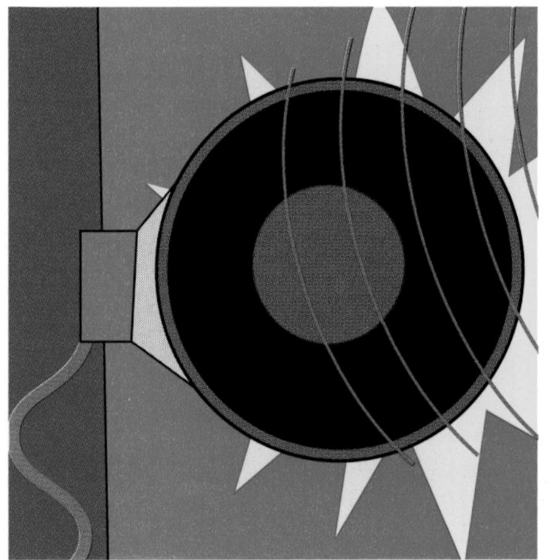

Analog versus Digital

FIRST-TIME VISITORS to a broadcast TV station are invariably amazed at the quality of the pictures they see on the station's TV monitors. The picture is incredibly sharp, crystal clear, and free of noise, ghosts, and other picture problems. You don't see it that way at home because of the noise and distortion introduced into the signal on its journey from the TV station to your set. If you own a camcorder, you've seen the same phenomenon at home. If you hook up your camcorder to your TV set, you'll see a very clear, noise-free picture. But if you record some footage on tape and play it back, it isn't quite as sharp and clear. The picture loses some of its quality in the recording and playback process.

Our radio, television, and telephone systems use analog signals to carry the picture and sound information. Analog signals aren't inherently inferior to digital signals; in fact, our current-day analog TV and audio equipment can produce pictures and sound of extraordinary quality. Far into our digital future, we'll still have analog equipment because the things we want to record—pictures and sound—are inherently analog.

An *analog signal* is a signal whose frequency and/or intensity is directly proportional—analogous—to the data that the signal represents. The problem with analog signals is that they are notoriously difficult to record and transmit intact. Small amounts of noise and distortion are introduced into the signal at each step of the way. Once an analog signal is damaged by noise and distortion, there's no way to restore it.

Some broadcast systems—notably over-the-air and cable television—require that a signal pass through many stages before it reaches its audience. By the time a TV picture goes from the camera to a video recorder to the studio to the transmitter to the cable TV system to your set, the accumulated noise and distortion really add up. The result is often a blurry, noisy picture.

Analog recording and playback equipment are major offenders in the noise and distortion department. That's why compact discs provide sound quality superior to records and tapes; CDs store music in a digital form and convert the digital information back to analog audio inside the CD player.

Transmission and distribution equipment is another major source of noise and distortion. Over-the-air broadcast TV is adversely affected by atmospheric conditions like lightning and rain, by signals reflected off of adjacent buildings, and even by airplanes passing overhead. Analog telephone *subscriber loops*—the connection between your home or office and the telephone company's switching equipment—use the same basic technology used in early Bell System telephones over 100 years ago! The subscriber loop can be adversely affected by thousands of things, including power tools and other electrical equipment, nearby radio and TV transmitters, and even by other subscriber loop cables—a condition known as *crosstalk*.

Digital transmission systems don't have these problems because they contain built-in error correction. Digital systems communicate by breaking down data to a simple "on" or "off" condition. If the data is damaged between two points, the system automatically retransmits the damaged data. Some digital systems also use a technique called *forward error correction*. This technique encodes the data so that if a few bits of data are lost in transmission, they can be reconstructed at the receiving end.

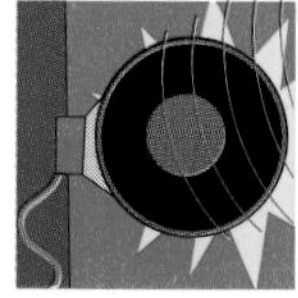

Fortunately, it's fairly simple to convert analog signals to digital and back again. Devices called *A/D converters* and *D/A converters* handle the dual tasks of analog-to-digital and digital-to-analog conversion. A/D and D/A converters have fallen drastically in price, thanks to their widespread use in CD players, computer sound systems, and digital cellular phones.

Digital Sampling

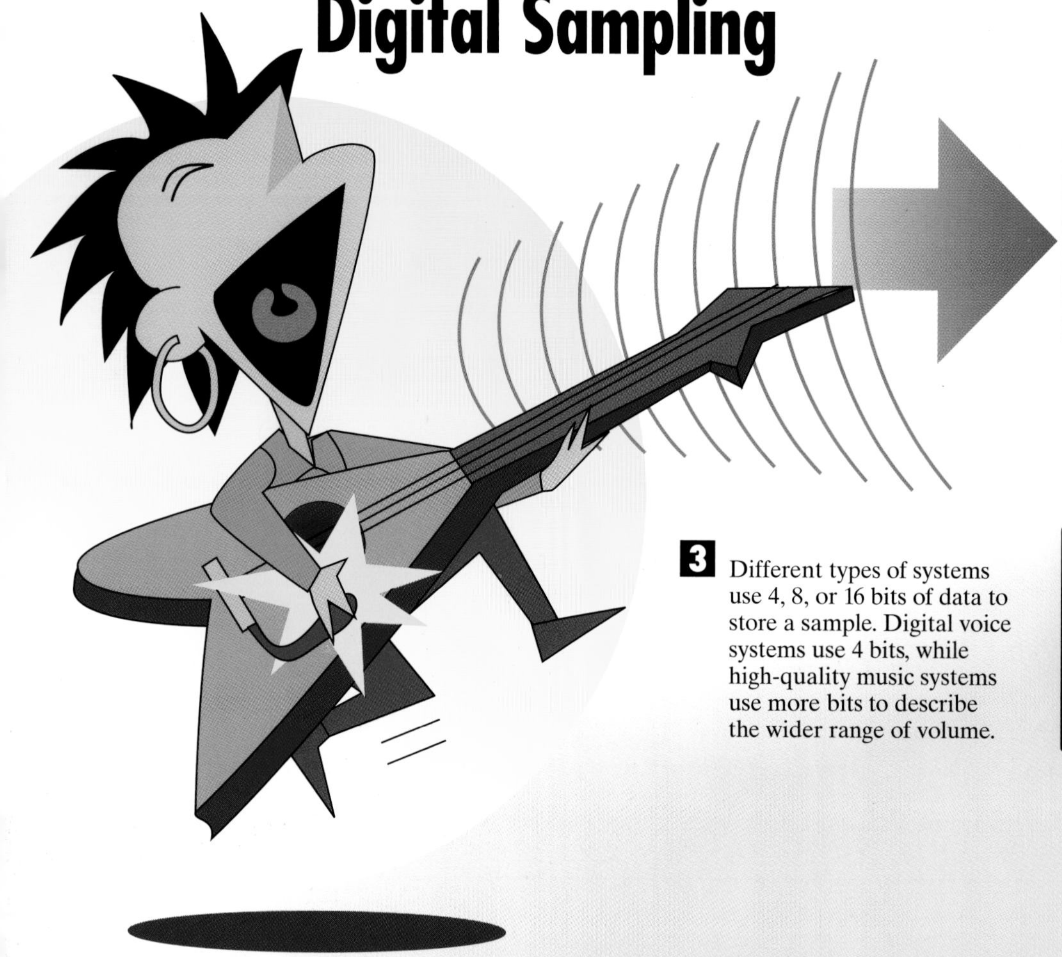

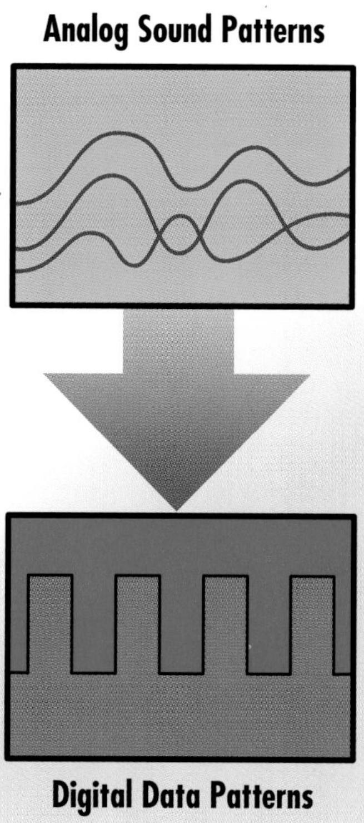

3 Different types of systems use 4, 8, or 16 bits of data to store a sample. Digital voice systems use 4 bits, while high-quality music systems use more bits to describe the wider range of volume.

1 How do complex sound patterns become marching bits of zeros and ones? The answer is *sampling*, a technique that takes tens of thousands of slices of sound per second and records them digitally. By making many samples, the digital system can create an excellent picture of the complex sound waveform.

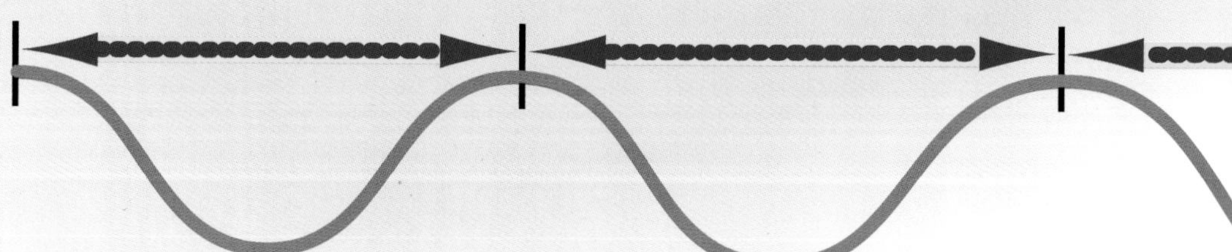

2 Each sample results in the creation of a string of zeros and ones containing information on the strength and frequency of the tone.

5 Some encoding schemes, such as the adaptive delta pulse code modulation (ADPCM), offer 3:1 data compression.

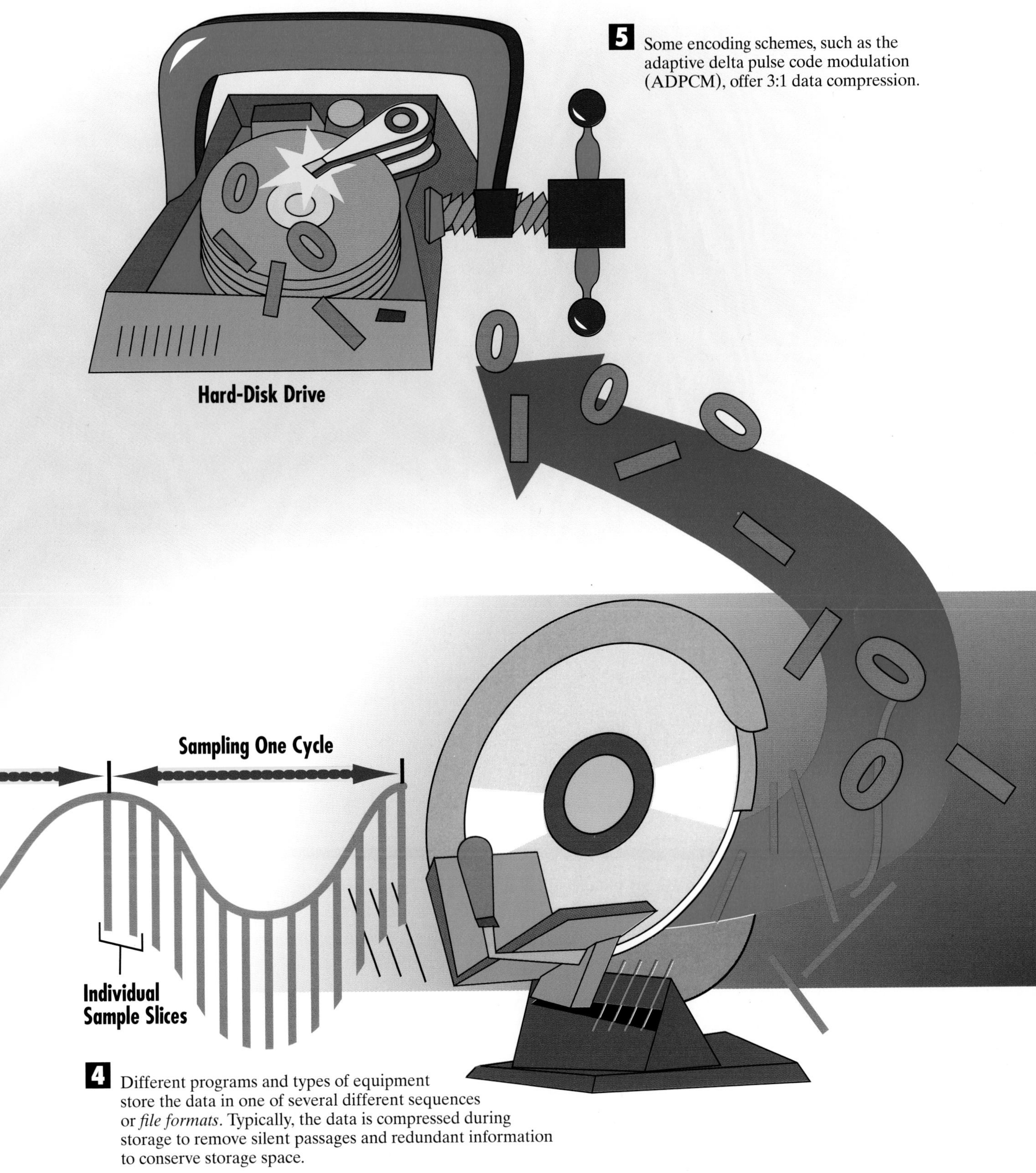

4 Different programs and types of equipment store the data in one of several different sequences or *file formats*. Typically, the data is compressed during storage to remove silent passages and redundant information to conserve storage space.

How Digital Audio Works

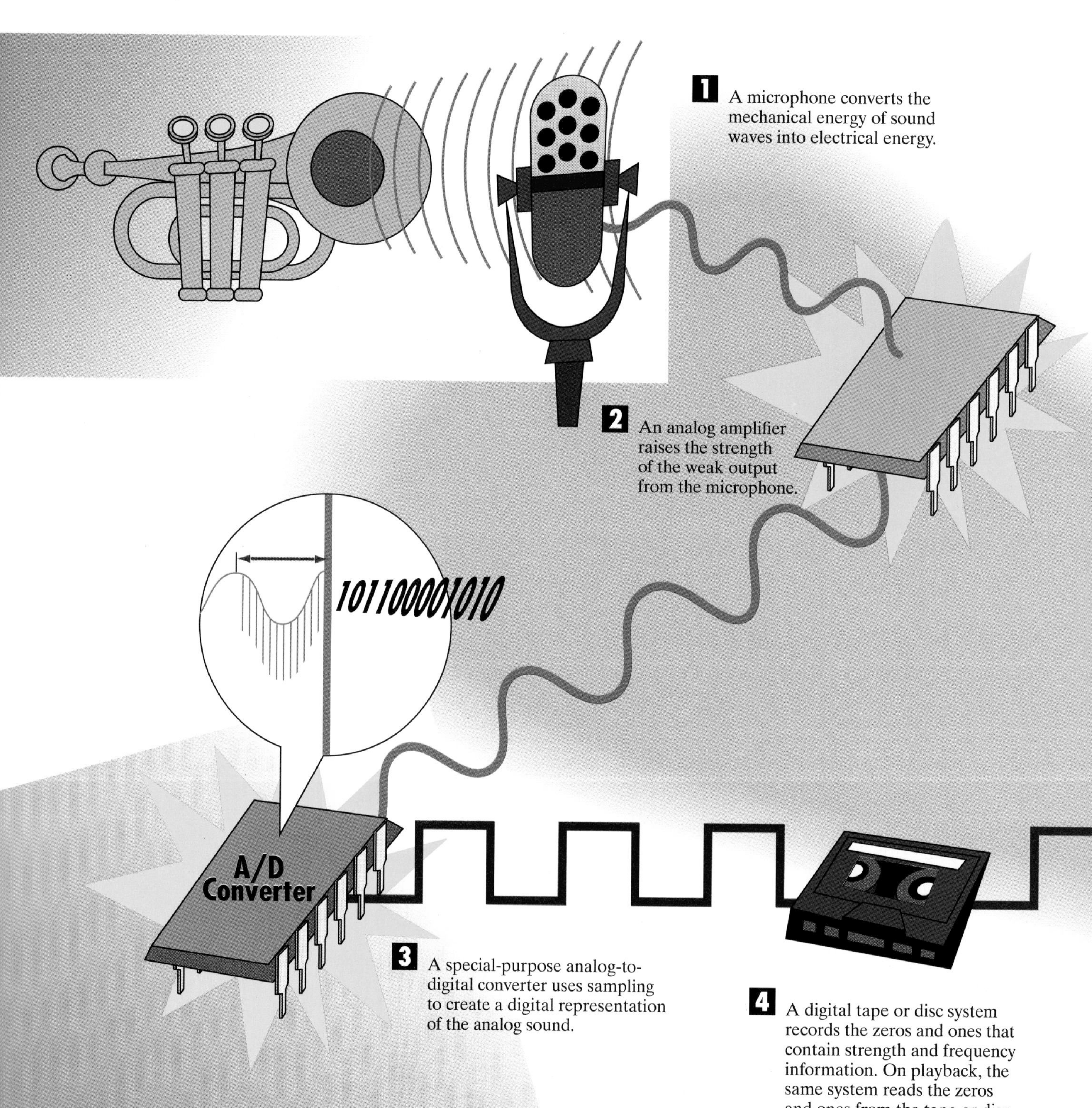

1 A microphone converts the mechanical energy of sound waves into electrical energy.

2 An analog amplifier raises the strength of the weak output from the microphone.

3 A special-purpose analog-to-digital converter uses sampling to create a digital representation of the analog sound.

4 A digital tape or disc system records the zeros and ones that contain strength and frequency information. On playback, the same system reads the zeros and ones from the tape or disc.

7 A speaker changes the analog electrical energy into mechanical energy, or sound waves.
6 A power transistor boosts the sound level so it can drive a loudspeaker.
D/A Converter
5 Digital data goes to a special-purpose device called a digital-to-analog converter. The digital-to-analog converter re-creates the analog sound from its digital representation.

The Telephone Network

WE AMERICANS LOVE our telephones so much that we put them everywhere—in our homes and offices, in our cars, on airplanes, in grocery stores, and on street corners. There are well over 150 million telephones in the United States alone. Behind the scenes is a complex maze of local telephone companies, long-distance carriers, satellites, fiber-optic cables, and millions of miles of wiring. These facilities belong to dozens of companies, including AT&T, MCI, GTE, and the former Bell System companies. Despite the complexity of the network, the system remains very easy to use. To make a call, you simply pick up the phone and dial a number.

AT&T is the nation's largest long-distance carrier and a major force in the telephone equipment business. In the process of building the telephone network, AT&T and many other companies devised thousands of very significant technical innovations. For example, scientists at AT&T's Bell Laboratories invented the transistor. The transistor is the building block for virtually all modern-day electronic equipment. The laser, essential to today's high-speed fiber-optic networks, is another Bell System invention. These two innovations have made our present-day telephone network more reliable, more efficient, and less expensive to operate.

As the telephone network grew at a phenomenal rate, telephone company engineers were faced with a nagging problem. The existing structure of the telephone trunk network—the lines that connect telephone company local switching offices with one another—were increasingly crowded. Each conversation required its own pair of wires. As telephone traffic increased, there simply weren't enough pairs of wires to meet demand. In some places, it was relatively easy to dig more tunnels and pull more wire from one central office to another. But in places like Manhattan and Los Angeles, digging more tunnels simply wasn't an option. The existing cable conduits—some built by Bell in the 1890s—were jam-packed full of wires. It would cost billions of dollars to tear up the streets to add more wire.

Telephone engineers faced another, more difficult problem. Electrical signals traveling over a wire lose some of their energy. As a result, a long telephone wire requires a device called a repeater every few miles or so along the wire. A *repeater* is essentially an amplifier. It takes a weak signal and makes it strong again, but at the cost of introducing noise and distortion into the signal. Wires traveling together tend to pass some of their lost energy into adjacent wires, creating interference between phone lines. To compound the problem, large electrical fields, like those produced by electric trains, elevators, and generators, force their way into telephone wires, further degrading the quality of the connection.

Most of these problems can be solved by a technique called *time division multiplexing*, or TDM. This technique first converts analog telephone audio into a series of digital pulses. Those digital pulses are joined together with the pulses from several other telephone conversations. TDM takes advantage of the fact that telephone conversations contain a lot of silence—one person talks while the other listens. By sending only the talking parts and leaving out the silent parts, TDM makes more efficient use of telephone lines. Using TDM, one pair of wires can carry several conversations. Like analog signals, digital signals are susceptible to noise and interference on the wire. However, digital repeaters can re-create an almost perfect copy of the original signal.

Thanks to the widespread use of TDM and other digital technologies, most of the long-haul telephone network is digital. To further solve the capacity problem, most telephone companies and long-distance carriers are installing fiber-optic cable instead of copper wire. A single fiber-optic cable can carry hundreds of conversations on a glass fiber the same size as a telephone wire.

So the good news is that the bulk of the telephone network is digital, and there's plenty of capacity on the network. The bad news is that the last mile from the telephone company office to our homes and businesses is still analog technology. While analog technology is perfectly acceptable for voice telephone conversations, it poses a serious bottleneck for digital information. If you want to connect your computer to another computer or information service, you'll have to use a modem. A modem takes digital data from a computer and converts it into a series of tones that can be transmitted over the voice telephone network—where, ironically, it is usually converted into digital form. Because of the limited bandwidth of an analog voice-grade telephone line, modems are relatively slow. Today's fastest modems achieve a data rate of about 28,000 bps—far too slow for full-motion video and hi-fi sound.

How did we get stuck in a technological stone age? As we've seen, the telephone companies had a pressing need to convert their interoffice lines to digital transmission. But until recently, there was very little demand for digital service from individual telephone customers. Bringing digital service to homes and small businesses is a difficult proposition. Most long-haul telephone cables travel through relatively wide-open spaces like railroad right-of-ways and along interstate highways, making it relatively easy to add new cables or replace existing ones. Local telephone cables run under or over every street and into every building in the country. Digital service will require replacing much of that cable with something other than telephone wire—a monumental undertaking.

Analog Telephones in a Digital World

Every home and office telephone is connected to a telephone company *central office* (CO). A pair of thin copper wires connects your phone to the CO. The wires carry analog audio signals to and from the CO.

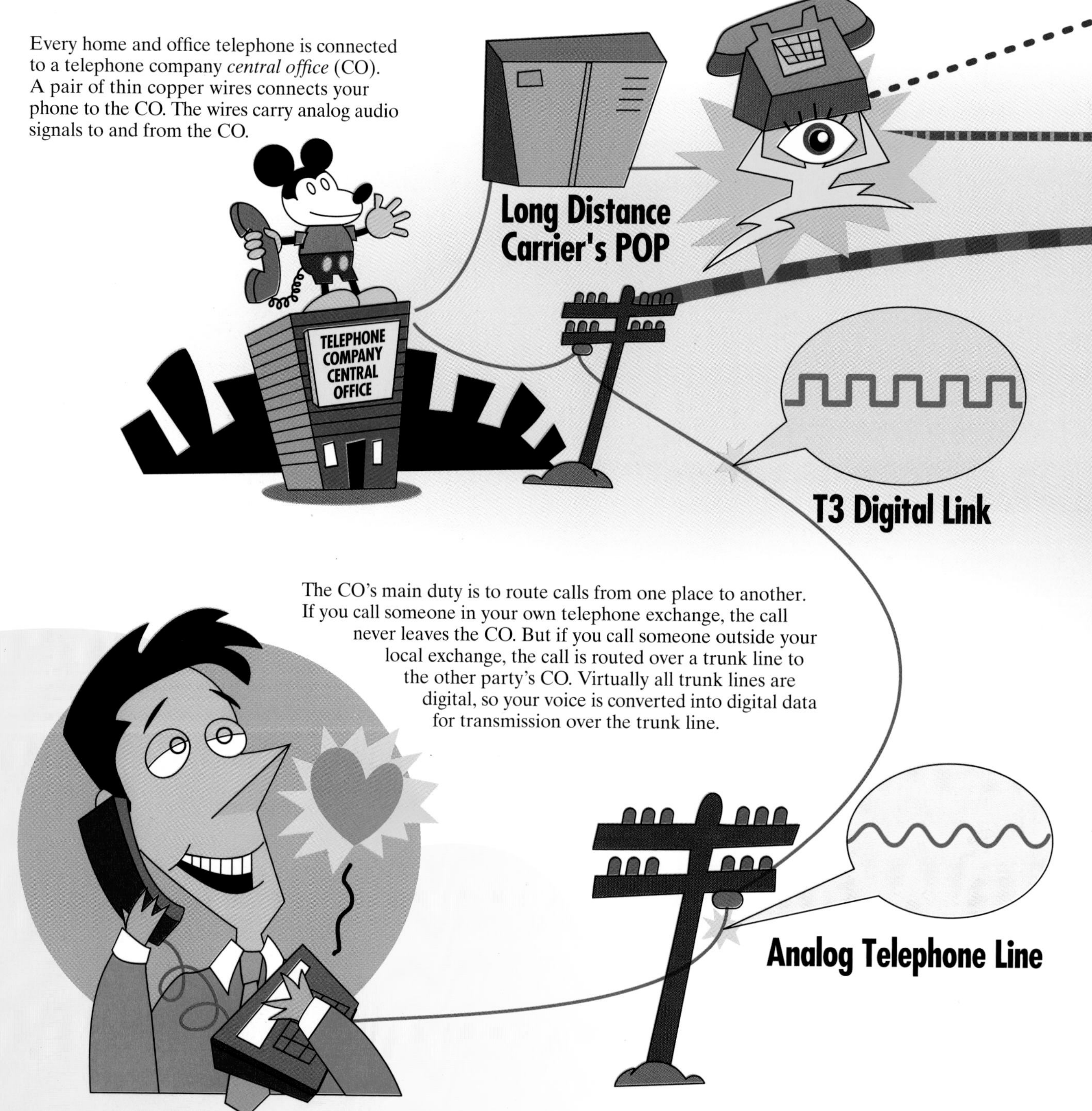

The CO's main duty is to route calls from one place to another. If you call someone in your own telephone exchange, the call never leaves the CO. But if you call someone outside your local exchange, the call is routed over a trunk line to the other party's CO. Virtually all trunk lines are digital, so your voice is converted into digital data for transmission over the trunk line.

If you make a long-distance call, the call is routed from your CO to your long-distance carrier's *point of presence* (POP). The long-distance carrier's own equipment routes the call to the POP nearest the party you are calling, where it travels to the called party's CO.

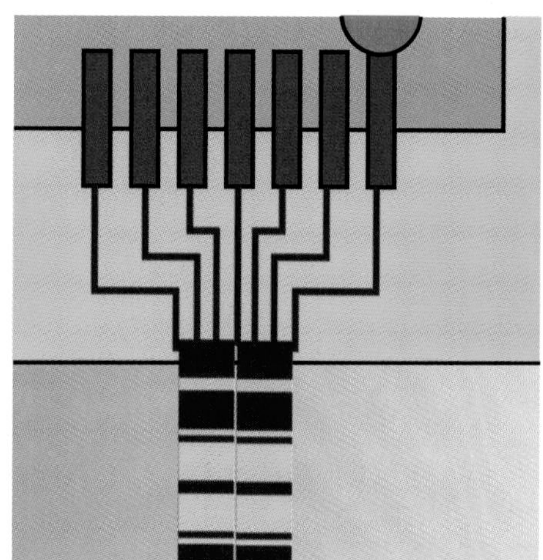

Digital Communications Techniques

THE OLD PROVERB "The Devil is in the details" applies aptly to digital networking when you consider the details of the way data moves over the information highway. However, once you understand a few basic concepts behind these details, you'll see that things are not as complex as you thought. In this chapter, we'll explain such imposing terms as ISDN, packet switching, and other digital transmission techniques you hear and read about. We'll also show you how those basic elements are related to one another.

In digital systems, information such as characters in text, dots in a picture, and the tones in music are encoded into binary patterns of zeros and ones. The encoding scheme is called a *data alphabet,* and the most common alphabet is the American Standard Code for Information Interchange (ASCII). Furthermore, a direct current voltage is used to signal the presence of a digital zero or a one. This process takes place on the cable that links the computers in a network. The actual voltage is similar in strength to the voltage you get from a car battery. For example, the adapter card that links a local area network (LAN) applies a positive or a negative voltage in the range of +15 to –15 volts to the network cable. And the transition between the voltage levels indicates a change from one binary state to the other.

The peak of each positive and negative cycle is flat, generating the picture of square waves. But as these square waves travel over the cable, various electrical characteristics of the cable and outside electrical noises reduce, deform, and obscure them. Faster signaling speeds make the situation more challenging because the higher speed decreases the duration between the square waves and makes it more difficult for receiving devices to accurately discriminate between them.

Generally, in communications systems there is an equation that requires you trade off transmission speed (also known as bandwidth) against distance and cost. If, for example, you increase the speed of the connection, then you must either decrease the distance or increase the cost of the equipment required to make the connection. Increasing the cost by investing in fiber-optic cabling can increase both the distance and speed. Stretching the length of a data connection from 100 yards to 10 miles significantly reduces the speed and increases the cost of equipment. Communications engineers have developed many techniques to send these digital signals farther and faster with fewer errors. You see these techniques as products and services you buy or lease, either directly or indirectly, from the companies selling the ramps to the digital highway.

Local area networks (LANs), by definition, remove distance from the equation because they typically exist in an area of a square mile or less. LAN systems typically operate at 10 or 16 megabits per second (Mbps)—speeds that can deliver audio and full-motion video in real time. Faster and more costly LAN services are capable of 100 and even 155 Mbps. Because they share a common cabling scheme, LANs are excellent multipoint systems. LANs use different schemes, such as Ethernet or TokenRing, to share the common cables. Ethernet uses a listen-before-transmit scheme, and Token-Ring uses a more rigidly controlled system based on timing.

Your PC, TV, or other portal onto the digital highway will use one of two types of connections. One type of service is called circuit switching. Your voice telephone is a circuit-switched device. When you dial a voice telephone call, you are programming a computer maintained by the telephone company. The computer reacts to your commands by connecting the line or circuit from your home or office to a circuit going to another premises. Digital circuit-switched systems, such as the Integrated Services Digital Network (ISDN) and Switched 56, work exactly the same way. Your computer or set-top box tells the telephone company's switch what connection to make, and the switch establishes the connection within milliseconds. While the connection is up, there is a dedicated pipeline between the two premises moving data at speeds of 128 kilobits per second (Kbps) for ISDN or even faster. When the computers finish transferring data, they hang up and the circuits are available for other calls.

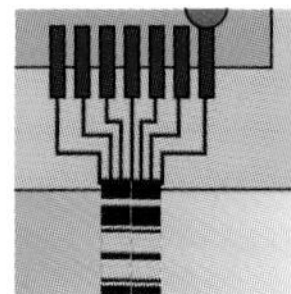

Circuit-switched services like ISDN do a great job of delivering some types of data. For example, they work well if you want to receive a broadcast with sound and video from an information and entertainment service. They also work well to link your office at home to your main office network system. In fact, many of the connections for the digital highway, particularly those delivered by telephone companies, will rely on ISDN. These circuit-switched digital services will carry both old-fashioned voice-only telephone calls and exotic new multimedia services. However, circuit-switched services have limitations when it comes to delivering multipoint communications connections—for example, it's difficult to do a three-way digital conference call over a circuit-switched system.

Packet switching is the other type of connection you will be able to use on the digital highway. This service is more useful for multipoint connectivity. When they communicate, computerized devices gather the digital zeros and ones that represent data into groups called *packets.* Each packet contains destination, origination, and error-checking information. Communications devices such as modems handle bits, which are the individual zeros and ones. But computer and communications programs process bits in packets, or groups. Sometimes they stream the packets over direct connections between communicating devices, but often they switch the packets across a complex web of interconnections.

In packet-switched systems, computers are maintained by a service provider. For example, a cable company, a power company, a satellite company, or a telephone company, may receive the packets your computer sends and switch them through a web of connections. The packet switches work like a railroad switching yard, in which trains are dispatched car-by-car. Each car is set on the right track to its destination—or perhaps on to yet another switching yard. Likewise, packet-switching handles the data packet-by-packet instead of connection-by-connection.

In addition to its multipoint capability, packet switching makes it easier and more economical to share high-speed ports among massive database computers. All of the modern information services such as CompuServe and the Internet use packet-switching technology.

You'll hear about different types of packet-switching services. For example, X.25 is an international standard for packet switching that is still widely used in Europe. The X.25 standards were rigorously engineered to ensure reliable delivery of data even over noisy connections. However, the reliability of X.25 imposes overhead in the communications circuits in terms of acknowledgment and error-handling messages and information.

In 1990, a newer technology called frame relay began to overtake X.25 in North America. High-quality connections in North America and smarter software in computers allowed the design of smaller frame relay packets that move data reliably and with more efficiency than X.25. Every vendor of wide area packet-switching services from CompuServe to Wiltel, Sprint, AT&T, and MCI can provide frame relay subscriber service at speeds of 1.544 Mbps and 2.048 Mbps.

The advantage of frame relay is that it makes the best use of the available bandwidth by packaging the data in variable-length packets for transmission across the network. Variable-length packets suit the bursty nature of computer data transmissions. Frame relay has less error-control than X.25, but it suits the current telephone system in North America.

LANs are the local distribution and information access point for millions of users. LAN file servers can download huge volumes of data from entertainment and information providers and hold them locally for faster and more economical sharing. LAN communications servers act as portals to costly communications links. Aside from speed, there is another major difference between long-distance digital connections and network connections. LAN connections are not switched between network nodes as they are in circuit- and packet-switched schemes.

Circuit Switching

The central office of every local telephone company is a computerized switch that works with other, similar switches to route and complete a call. That's how we get the term "circuit switching."

CENTRAL OFFICE SWITCHES

Digital access equipment connected to a router calls the central office switch. ISDN equipment uses a separate 16 Mbps channel for fast-call setup. Other switched services use standard dialing tones.

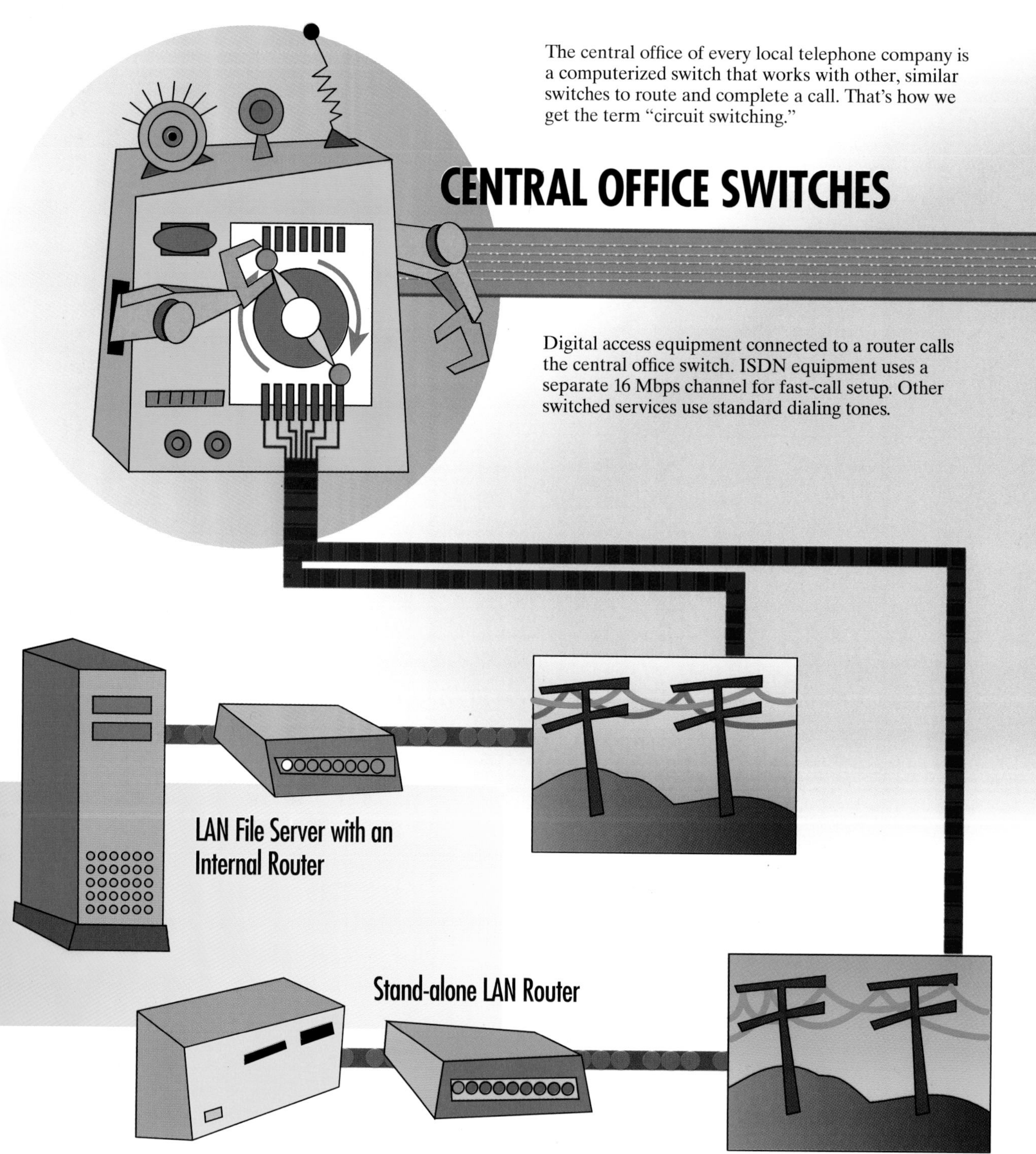

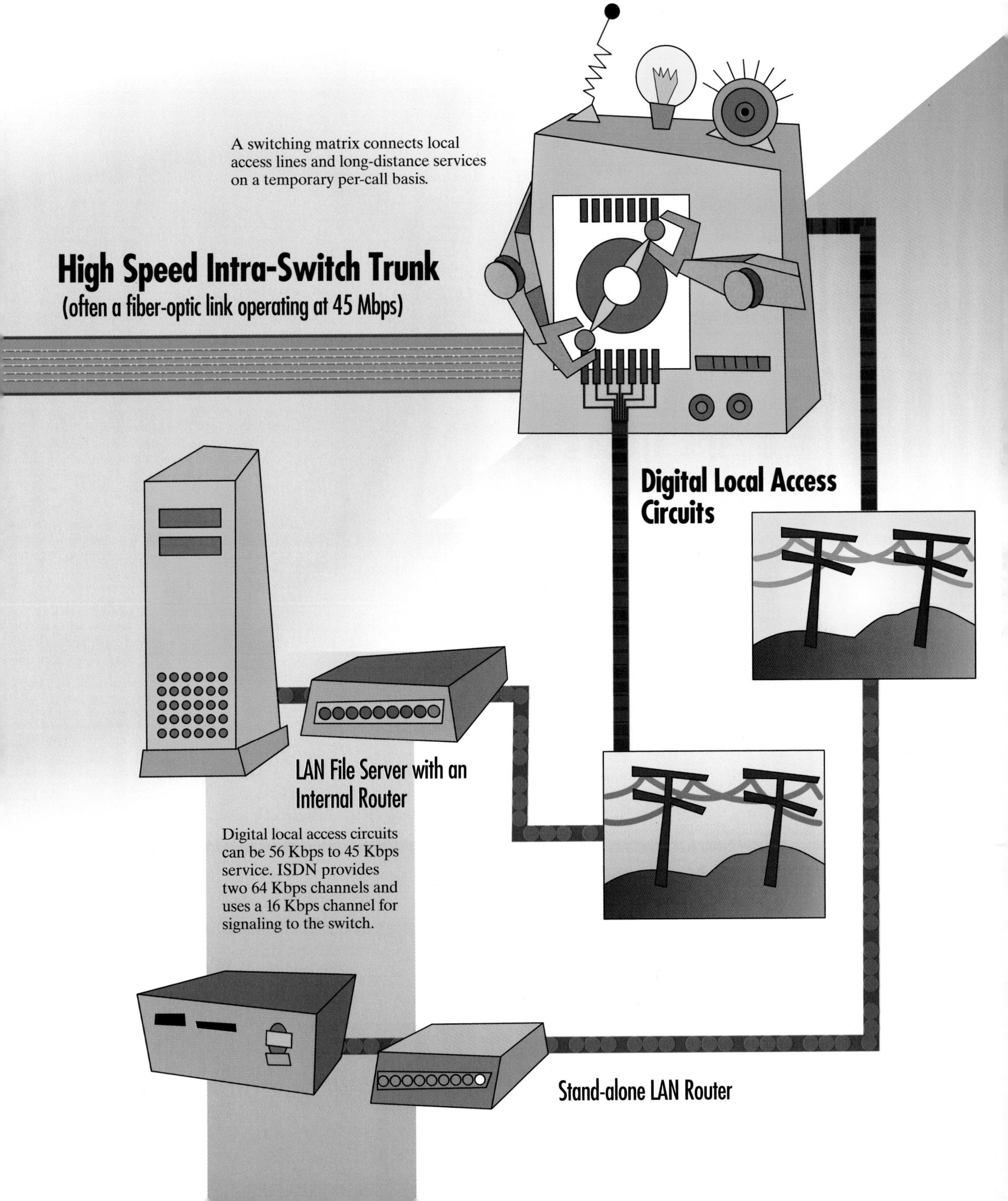

A switching matrix connects local access lines and long-distance services on a temporary per-call basis.

High Speed Intra-Switch Trunk
(often a fiber-optic link operating at 45 Mbps)

Digital Local Access Circuits

LAN File Server with an Internal Router

Digital local access circuits can be 56 Kbps to 45 Kbps service. ISDN provides two 64 Kbps channels and uses a 16 Kbps channel for signaling to the switch.

Stand-alone LAN Router

Packet-Switched Systems

Packet-switched systems provide an important way to move data economically and reliably between multiple network locations. The network's computerized switches wrap the data that is in transit inside an envelope containing destination, routing, and error-control information. Within milliseconds, the switch determines the routes and actions to take for each packet.

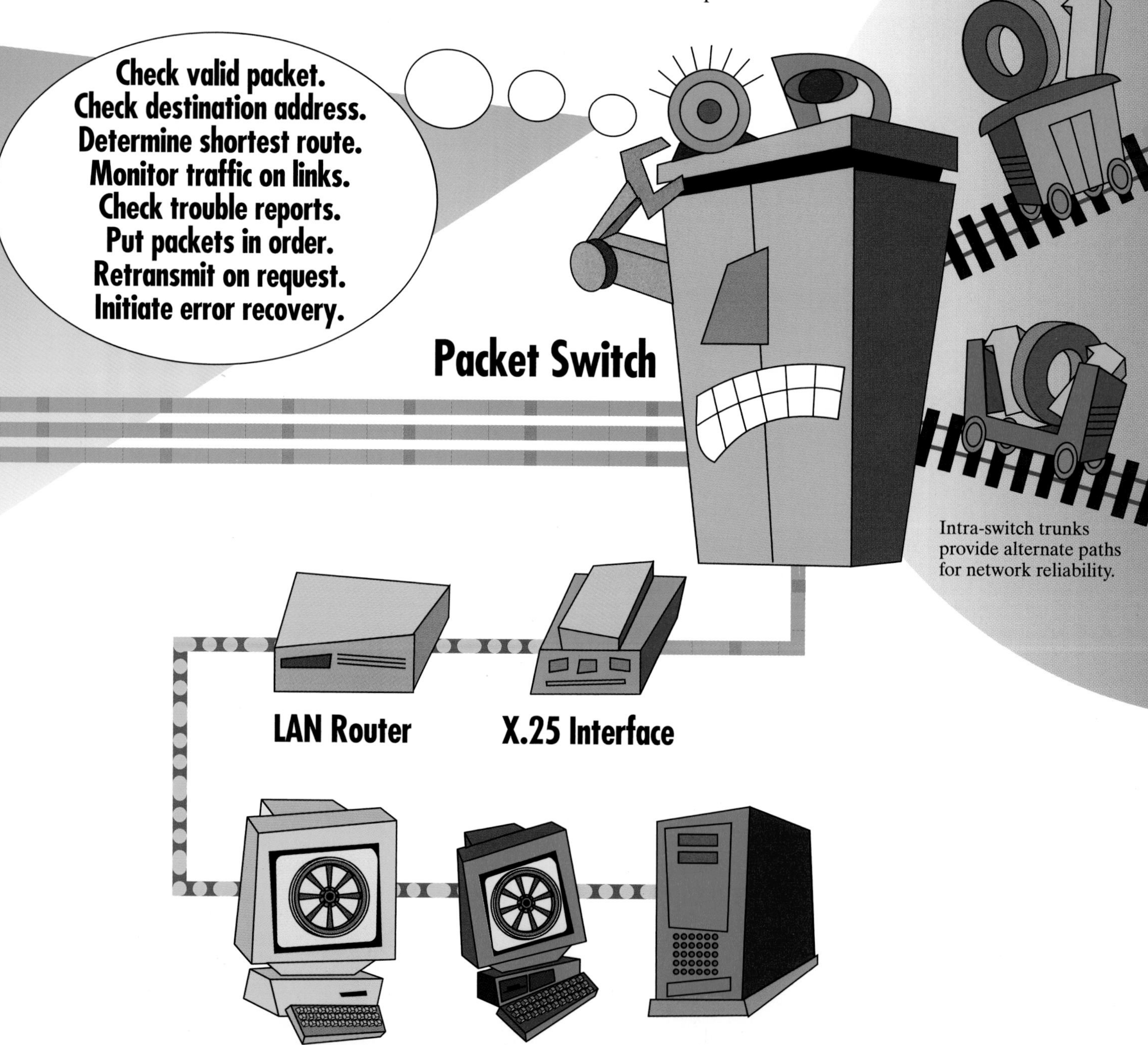

Intra-switch trunks provide alternate paths for network reliability.

Packet Switch

Typical rates for digital access lines are 19.2 Kbps to 1.544 Mbps.

Digital Access Line

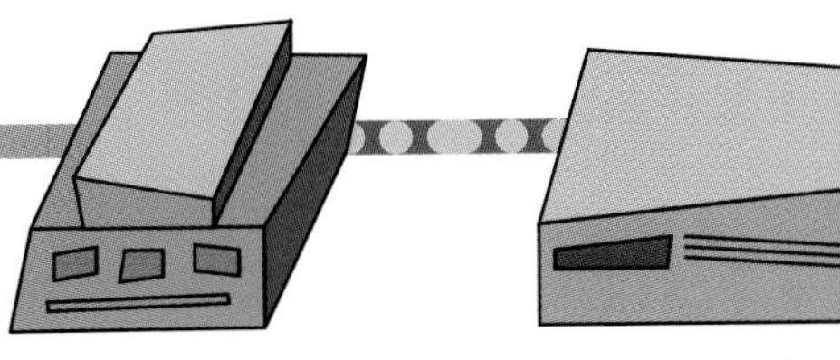

X.25 Interface

LAN Router

Each packet contains addressing, routing, time, checksum, and other network information. Frame relay packets contain less recovery information. If a packet is lost or damaged, higher-level programs retransmit.

Digital Access Line

X.25 Interface

LAN Router

Packet Switch

Local Area Network (LAN) Connections

Modern LAN adapters come with software that automatically integrates them into the computer, avoiding tricky installation problems.

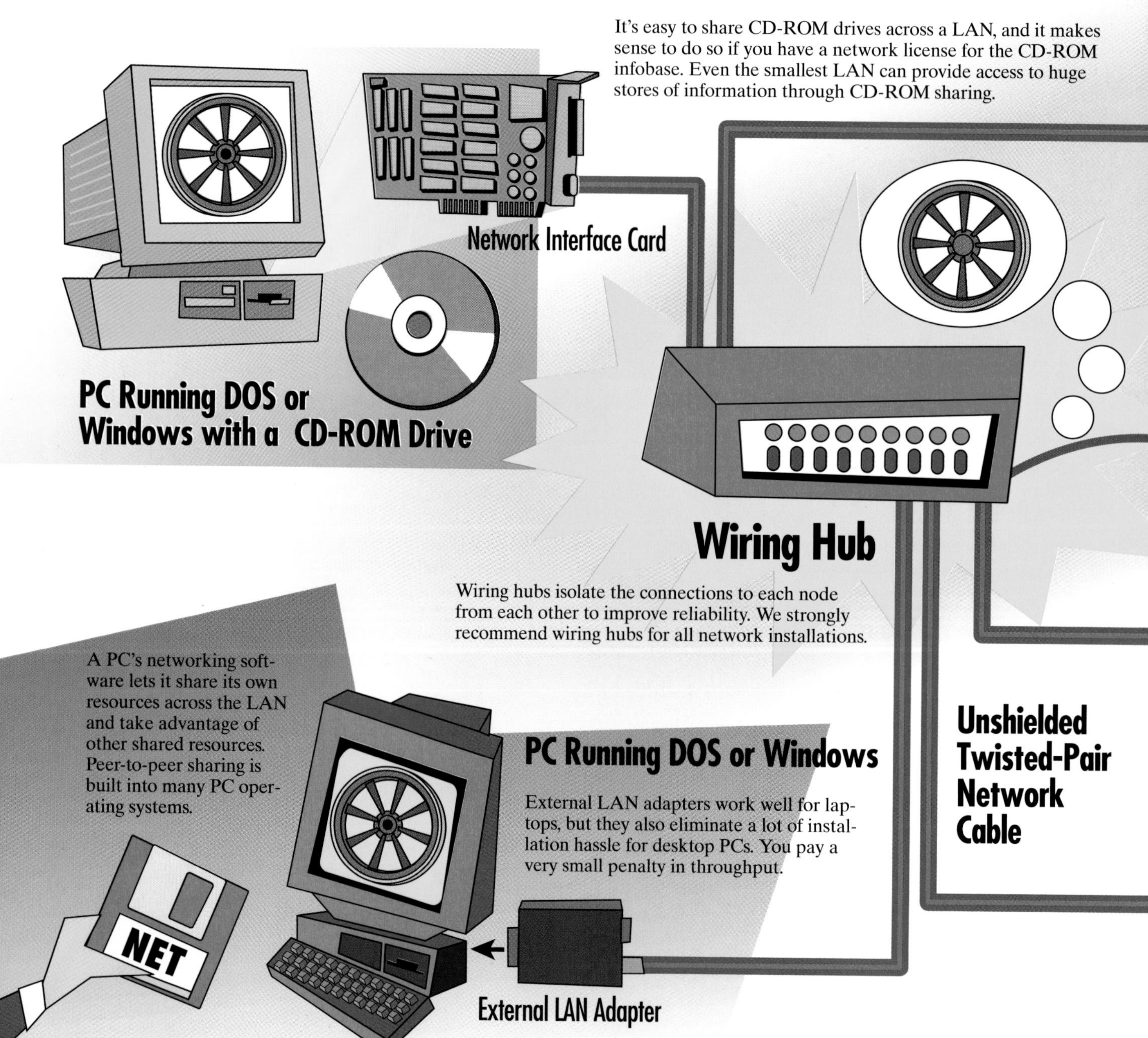

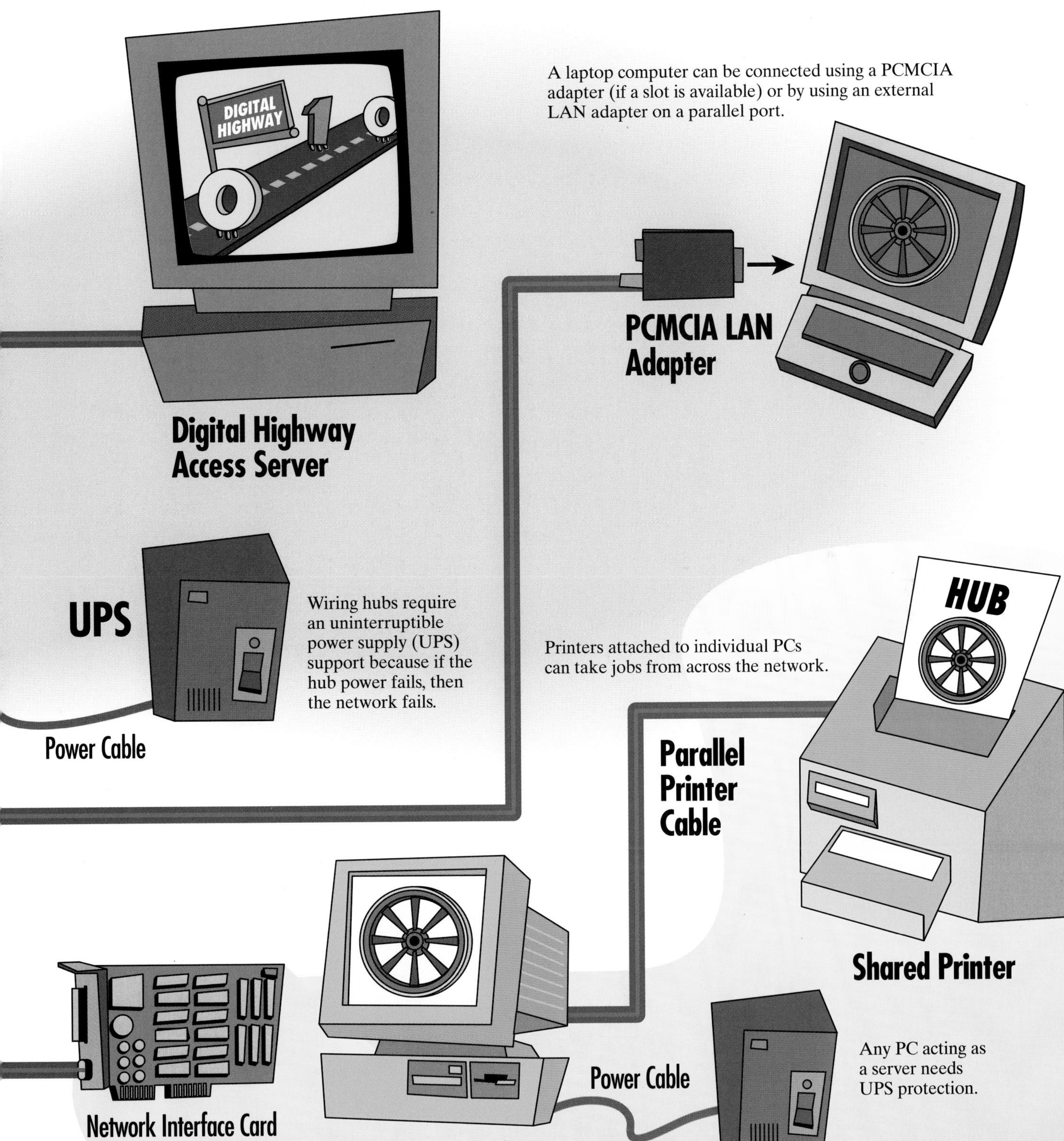
DIGITAL HIGHWAY
Digital Highway Access Server
A laptop computer can be connected using a PCMCIA adapter (if a slot is available) or by using an external LAN adapter on a parallel port.
PCMCIA LAN Adapter
UPS
Wiring hubs require an uninterruptible power supply (UPS) support because if the hub power fails, then the network fails.
Power Cable
Printers attached to individual PCs can take jobs from across the network.
HUB
Parallel Printer Cable
Shared Printer
Network Interface Card
Power Cable
Any PC acting as a server needs UPS protection.

How an Organization Links to the Digital Highway

The digital highway will take many paths. People will connect to each other and to sources of information through telephone services, wireless communications, digital signals carried over power lines, and satellite links. Each organization or family will choose the most economical links for their needs, and a variety of carriers will serve every community.

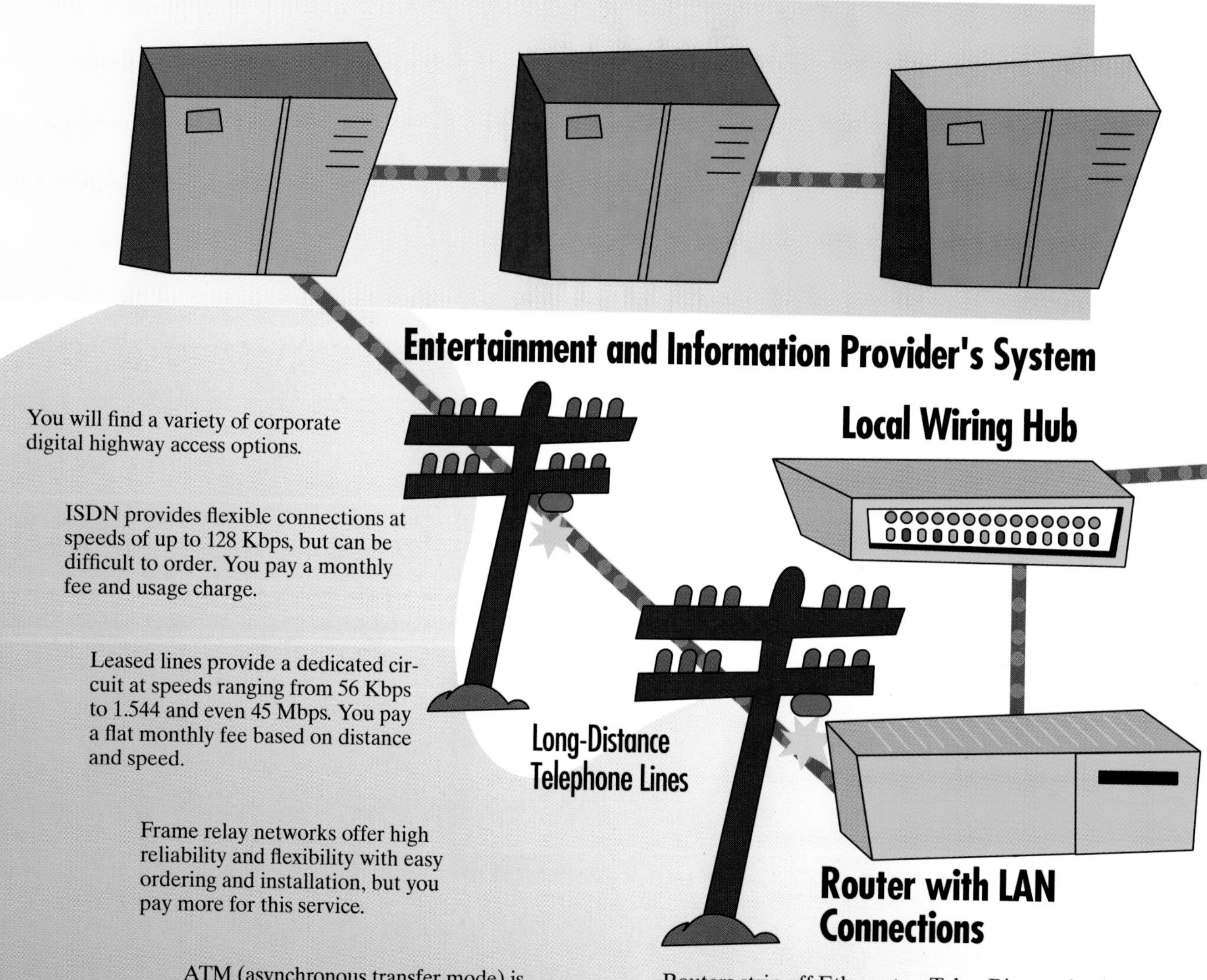

You will find a variety of corporate digital highway access options.

ISDN provides flexible connections at speeds of up to 128 Kbps, but can be difficult to order. You pay a monthly fee and usage charge.

Leased lines provide a dedicated circuit at speeds ranging from 56 Kbps to 1.544 and even 45 Mbps. You pay a flat monthly fee based on distance and speed.

Frame relay networks offer high reliability and flexibility with easy ordering and installation, but you pay more for this service.

ATM (asynchronous transfer mode) is an emerging technology for fast signaling with little delay—a feature needed for video+voice transmissions.

Routers strip off Ethernet or TokenRing packaging to improve efficiency over expensive long-distance links. Intelligent routers learn the connection paths to distant nodes and only pass necessary traffic.

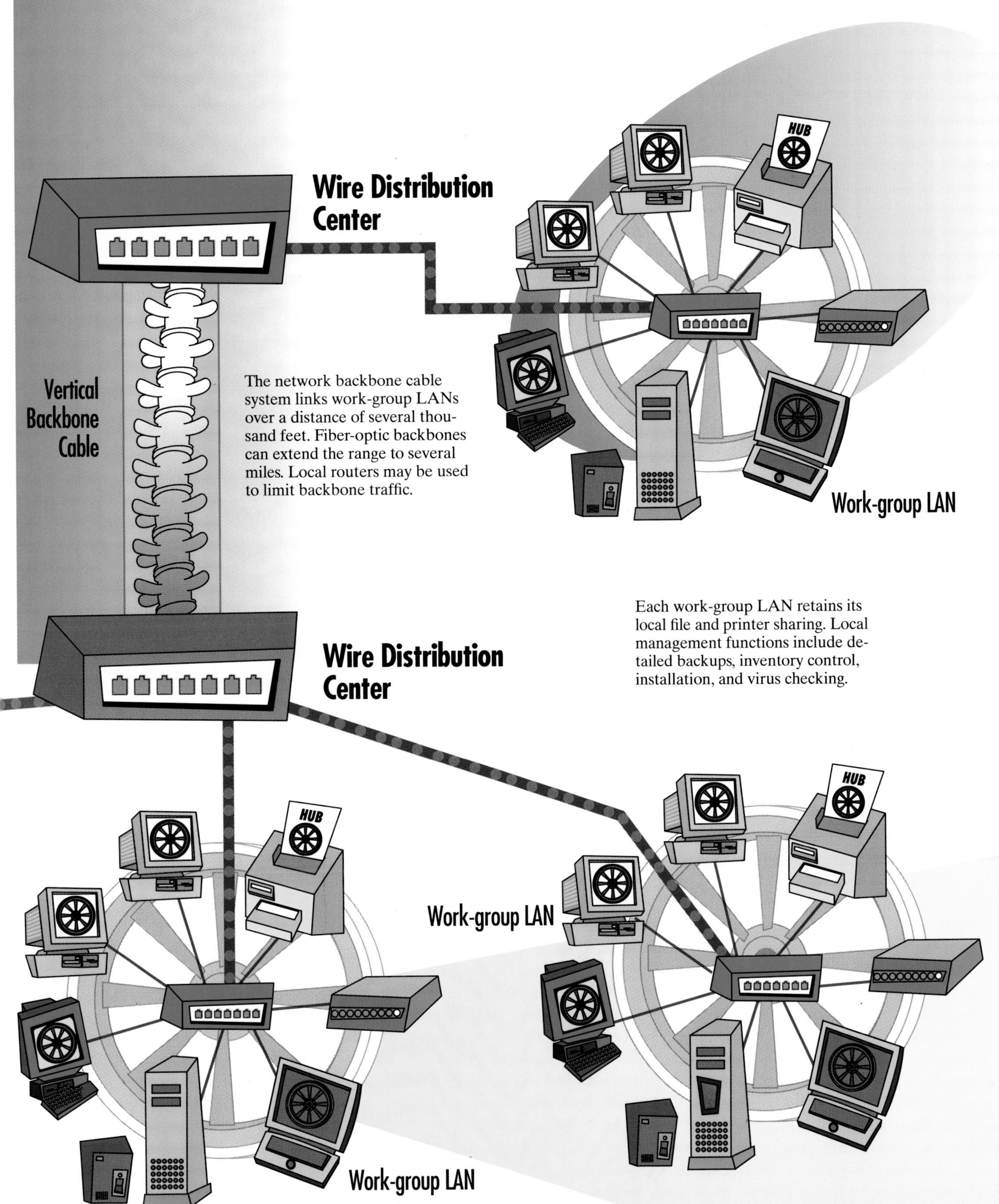

The network backbone cable system links work-group LANs over a distance of several thousand feet. Fiber-optic backbones can extend the range to several miles. Local routers may be used to limit backbone traffic.

Each work-group LAN retains its local file and printer sharing. Local management functions include detailed backups, inventory control, installation, and virus checking.

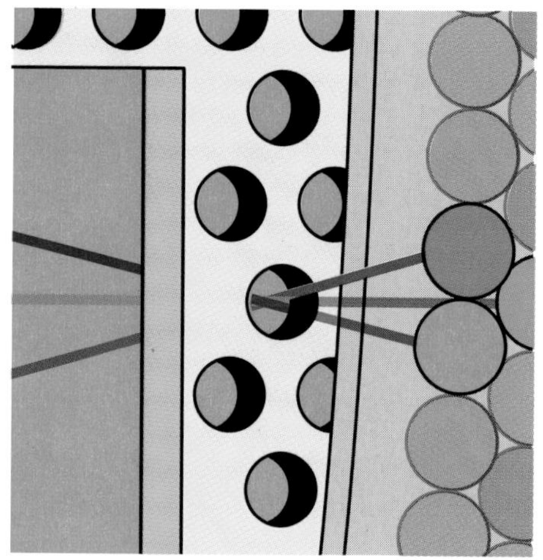

CHAPTER 16

Analog Television Standards

EACH YEAR, THOUSANDS of electronics equipment manufacturers, retailers, and distributors attend the giant Consumer Electronics Show (CES) in Las Vegas. At the show, the world's consumer electronic equipment manufacturers trot out their latest and greatest TVs, VCRs, and other home electronic gear. A few weeks after the CES show, those new products begin to appear in your local retail stores. Every year, the makers of TV sets promise sharper, clearer pictures, with better sound, more features, and fancier remote controls. The manufacturers deliver on that promise—to a point. For example, color TV technology hasn't changed much since the first color program, which aired in 1964—an episode of NBC's "Bonanza."

Our television system is governed by a set of standards developed primarily by RCA. In 1953, these standards were approved by the Federal Communications Commission (FCC) and adopted by the *National Television Standards Committee* (NTSC). However, full-time network color broadcasting didn't happen until 1964. Even then, color sets were expensive and troublesome. The picture was often muddy and washed-out, with limited contrast and pale colors. Since then, advances in TV manufacturing and in camera technology have taken NTSC about as far as it will go. Our current NTSC equipment is about as good as NTSC can be.

The NTSC color TV specification determines the electronic signals that make up a color TV picture, and it also establishes a method for broadcasting those pictures over the air. The NTSC color TV standards are themselves based on earlier monochrome (black-and-white) TV standards devised in the early 1940s. The current NTSC video standard calls for a picture consisting of 525 horizontal lines, transmitted at the rate of 30 pictures, or *frames*, per second. Forty of those 525 lines are used for signal synchronization and other purposes, leaving about 485 active lines on the screen. The more lines, the sharper the picture. Back in the '60s, 25-inch TV sets were the largest available, and 485 lines looks acceptably sharp on a 25-inch screen. But on today's large-screen TVs, NTSC pictures look a bit grainy and coarse.

NTSC defines a 4:3 horizontal to vertical size ratio, called the *aspect ratio*. This ratio was chosen out of convenience back in the '40s and '50s. At that time, all picture tubes were round. The almost-square 4:3 ratio made good use of round picture tubes, but it poses problems for television broadcasters when they show wide-screen movies. They can *pan and scan*, or move the active area of the picture to show the most important part of the whole picture. However, this technique can be very distracting because the camera appears to move almost constantly—sort of like watching a movie shot from a roller coaster. A second technique uses a special *anamorphic* lens that squeezes the picture horizontally, allowing the full width of the film to appear on the TV screen. Unfortunately, anamorphic lenses make John Wayne look like an alien from *Close Encounters of the Third Kind*. A third technique, *letterboxing*, is often used on rental videos. Using this technique, the entire width of the film appears on the screen—but the vertical size is reduced. Black bands appear above and below the active picture area. Letterboxing is okay if you're watching on a large screen, but the small size can be disconcerting on smaller TVs. As we'll see in the next chapter, one of the major improvements promised by the next generation of televisions is a higher aspect ratio. The wider screen format will allow viewing of wide-screen movies with no compromises.

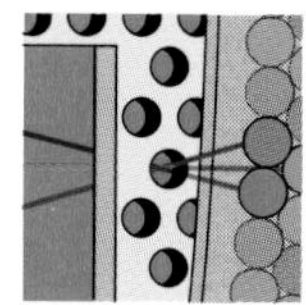

NTSC is an analog system, which is perhaps its biggest shortcoming. Under this system, video signals degrade quickly in adverse conditions. Even a small amount of noise and distortion can produce a noticeable decrease in picture sharpness; most of this signal degradation occurs along the path the picture travels from the studio to your TV. On the other hand, digital signals are nearly immune to interference and degradation, as we mentioned in Chapter 13. Digital TV is the topic of the next chapter.

There are two other major color TV standards in use today. The English/German *PAL* (Phase Alternation by Line) system is used in the United Kingdom, Western Europe, Australia, and Africa. The French *SECAM* (Systeme Electronique Couleur Avec Memoire) system is used in France and the former French colonies. A modified version of SECAM is used in Russia and the former Soviet-allied countries. Both the PAL and SECAM systems are fundamentally similar to NTSC, but PAL and SECAM use 625 lines at 25 frames per second.

The PAL and SECAM standards produce a sharper picture than NTSC, but have an annoying flicker due to the slower frame rate. American visitors to Europe are always amazed at the sharpness of PAL and SECAM, and Europeans often remark that American TV (at least the TV picture itself) doesn't give them a headache. In any case, TV programs produced in America must be converted into PAL and/or SECAM for distribution overseas, and vice versa. The conversion process detracts slightly from the image quality, and converted video often has a jerky, old-time-movie look to it. In addition, videotapes recorded in one format cannot be played back in another. PAL and SECAM share NTSC's 4:3 aspect ratio.

All three of these standards—NTSC, PAL, and SECAM—were designed for over-the-air broadcast TV. Back in Chapter 1, we talked about bandwidth—and bandwidth is what color TV likes best. An NTSC picture with sound occupies 6 MHz of frequency spectrum—enough bandwidth for 600 AM radio stations, 25 FM stations, or 2,222 voice-grade telephone lines!

How a Color Television Camera Works

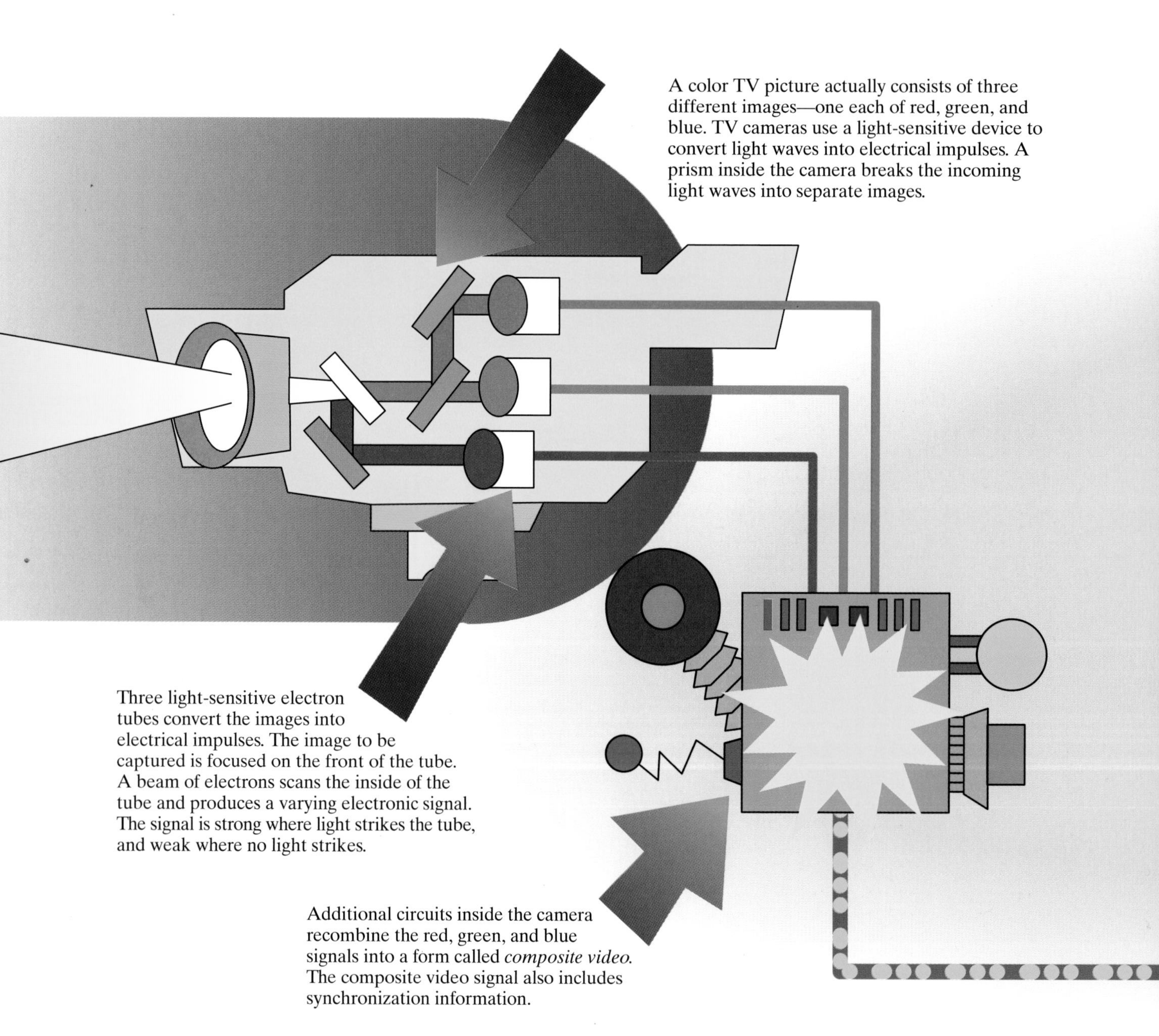

A color TV picture actually consists of three different images—one each of red, green, and blue. TV cameras use a light-sensitive device to convert light waves into electrical impulses. A prism inside the camera breaks the incoming light waves into separate images.

Three light-sensitive electron tubes convert the images into electrical impulses. The image to be captured is focused on the front of the tube. A beam of electrons scans the inside of the tube and produces a varying electronic signal. The signal is strong where light strikes the tube, and weak where no light strikes.

Additional circuits inside the camera recombine the red, green, and blue signals into a form called *composite video.* The composite video signal also includes synchronization information.

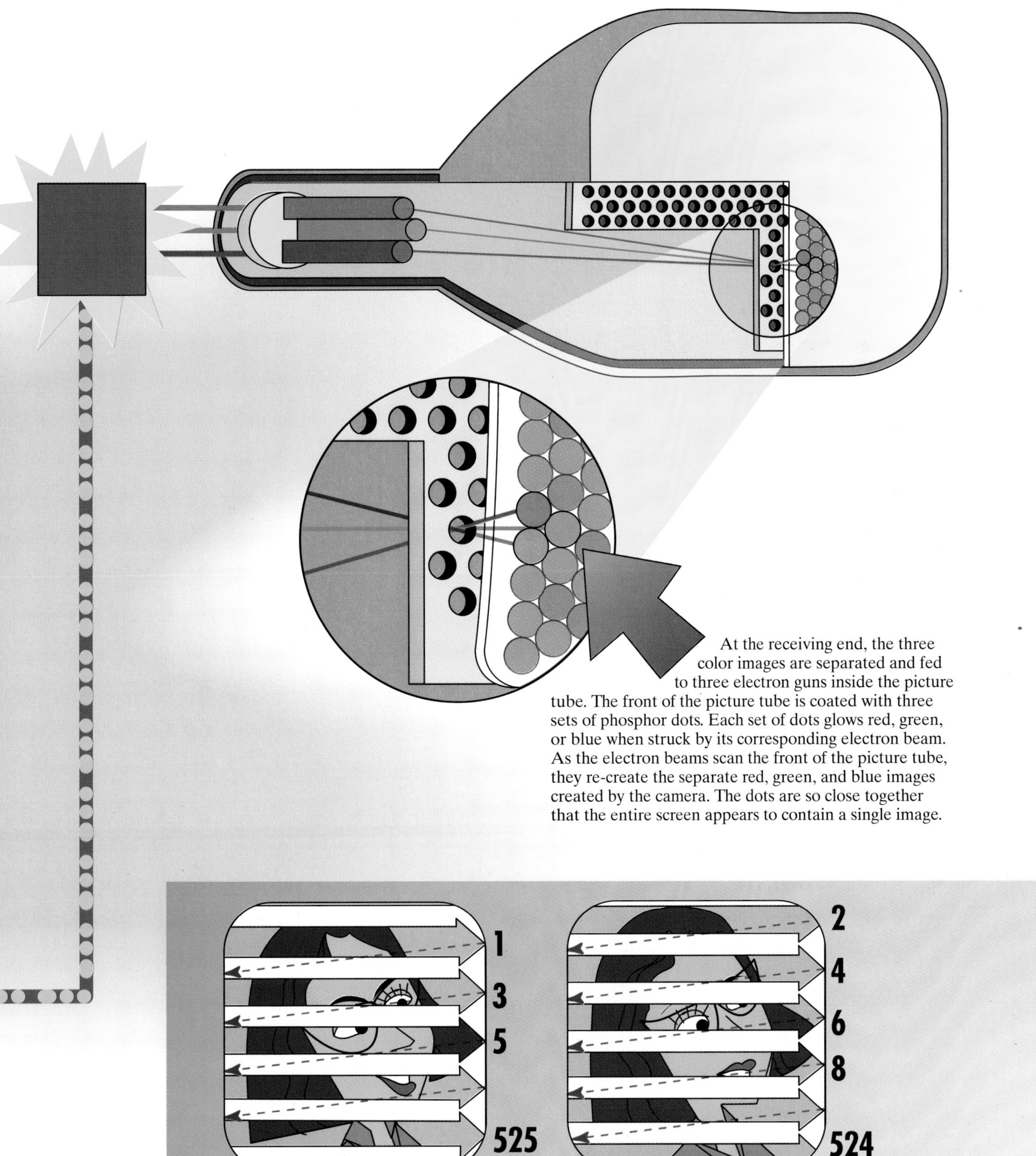

At the receiving end, the three color images are separated and fed to three electron guns inside the picture tube. The front of the picture tube is coated with three sets of phosphor dots. Each set of dots glows red, green, or blue when struck by its corresponding electron beam. As the electron beams scan the front of the picture tube, they re-create the separate red, green, and blue images created by the camera. The dots are so close together that the entire screen appears to contain a single image.

HDTV: The Digital Television Standard

WHEN OUR CURRENT analog NTSC color TV standards were created back in the 1950s, there were only two major players in the television industry—CBS and RCA. RCA's system was superior in many ways to the CBS system and had the added bonus of being compatible with earlier black-and-white TV standards. As a result, the RCA system won approval from the Federal Communications Commission (FCC) as the nation's color TV standard.

A great deal has changed since then. In the early days of television, virtually all television equipment—everything from the camera to the transmitter to the TV sets themselves—was made by RCA, General Electric, or a handful of smaller American companies. Today, the reverse is true. RCA and GE abandoned the TV studio equipment business in the 1970s, and Sony, Panasonic, and dozens of other Asian electronics firms have all but taken over the TV receiver business.

Given the Japanese dominance in the TV business, it may come as a surprise to hear that the new, digital High Definition Television (HDTV) standard recently approved by the FCC was created by a consortium of primarily American companies. The HDTV "Grand Alliance"—the digital counterpart to the NTSC of 40 years ago—was formed by AT&T, General Instrument (a major vendor of cable TV equipment), Zenith, the Massachusetts Institute of Technology, Thomson Consumer Electronics (France), Philips Consumer Electronics (Holland), and the David Sarnoff Research Center.

Why were no Japanese firms involved? Because the Japanese thought they had a head start in HDTV. While the Japanese firms have a large share of the U.S. market, the domestic Japanese market is still the most important to them. The Japanese have had broadcast HDTV for several years now, but the Japanese HDTV system is analog. Consequently, Japanese HDTV expertise is focused on a system that most U.S. TV experts consider obsolete.

The U.S. digital HDTV standard allows broadcasters to use any of seven formats, and all digital HDTV sets must be able to reproduce any of these formats. The highest resolution standard calls for a screen 1,920 pixels across by 1,080 lines vertically, with a frame rate of 60 frames per second (fps). Other, less technically demanding formats will provide either 1,920 by 1,080 screens with a frame rate of fewer than 60 fps, or 1,280 by 720 screens at 24, 30, or 60 fps. The aspect ratio—the ratio of width to height—of all seven formats is 16:9 or 1.78, providing a much wider picture than NTSC's 4:3 or 1.33.

The Grand Alliance standards also specify how the signal will be transmitted over broadcast and cable TV. The HDTV standard uses data compression techniques to squeeze 21.5 Mbps of data into a standard 6 MHz television broadcast channel.

Because cable TV didn't exist when the NTSC specifications were created, there were no special provisions for cable TV. Cable is inherently less susceptible to noise and interference than broadcast TV, and the HDTV specification takes this into account. HDTV cable transmissions can utilize an additional feature that packs 43 Mbps into a single 6 MHz cable channel. This allows cable operators to transmit two HDTV channels in the space currently used by one NTSC channel.

While HDTV isn't compatible with NTSC, HDTV stations will use the same 6 MHz radio spectrum bandwidth as NTSC broadcast stations. This allows HDTV stations to coexist with current broadcast TV stations—something the analog Japanese HDTV system can't do.

In addition to startling picture clarity and sharpness, HDTV will provide six channels of CD-quality sound. The six channels will allow for full surround-sound as well as multilingual stereo broadcasts.

And now for the bad news. HDTV will be expensive, at least initially. Estimated costs for first-generation HDTV sets range from $2,000 to $7,000 and up. Most of the cost of the early sets will be in the picture tube—HDTV sets require first-quality tubes. Once HDTV gets rolling, prices will fall like those of most other consumer electronic items.

Many industry analysts see HDTV as a chance for the American TV industry to regain its former glory. A typical HDTV set will be as much a computer as it is a television. The United States has long had a lead in small computer technology, and this may give U.S. TV makers a much-needed head start. HDTV sets will need lots of microprocessors and memory chips. If HDTV is a success, it will be a boon for American semiconductor makers. Because Japanese home-market HDTV sets won't work in the United States, the Japanese set makers don't have any particular advantage, even though they've enjoyed a head start with HDTV. The HDTV playing field is level—at least for the time being.

Inside a Digital TV

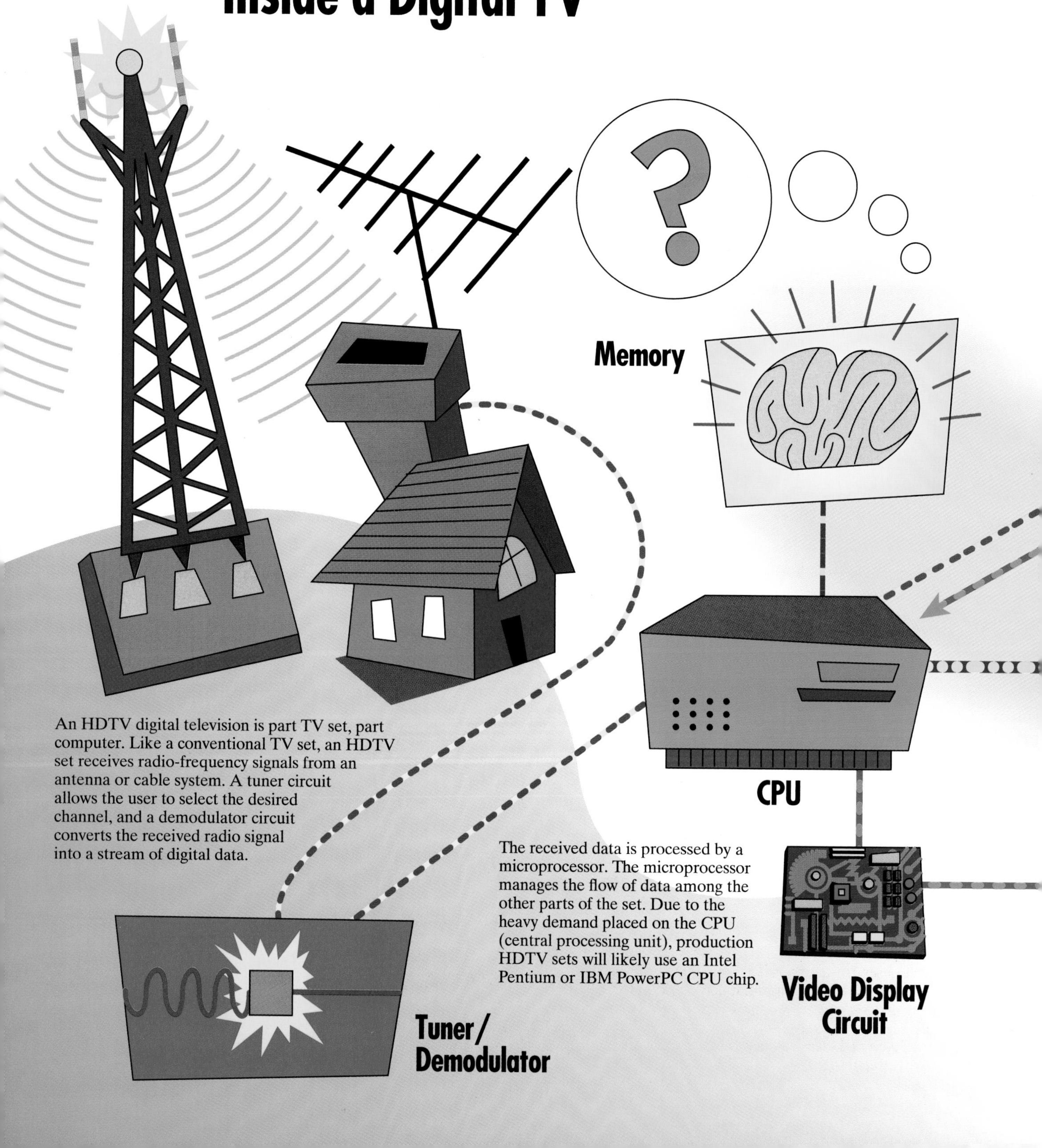

An HDTV digital television is part TV set, part computer. Like a conventional TV set, an HDTV set receives radio-frequency signals from an antenna or cable system. A tuner circuit allows the user to select the desired channel, and a demodulator circuit converts the received radio signal into a stream of digital data.

The received data is processed by a microprocessor. The microprocessor manages the flow of data among the other parts of the set. Due to the heavy demand placed on the CPU (central processing unit), production HDTV sets will likely use an Intel Pentium or IBM PowerPC CPU chip.

Memory

CPU

Video Display Circuit

Tuner/ Demodulator

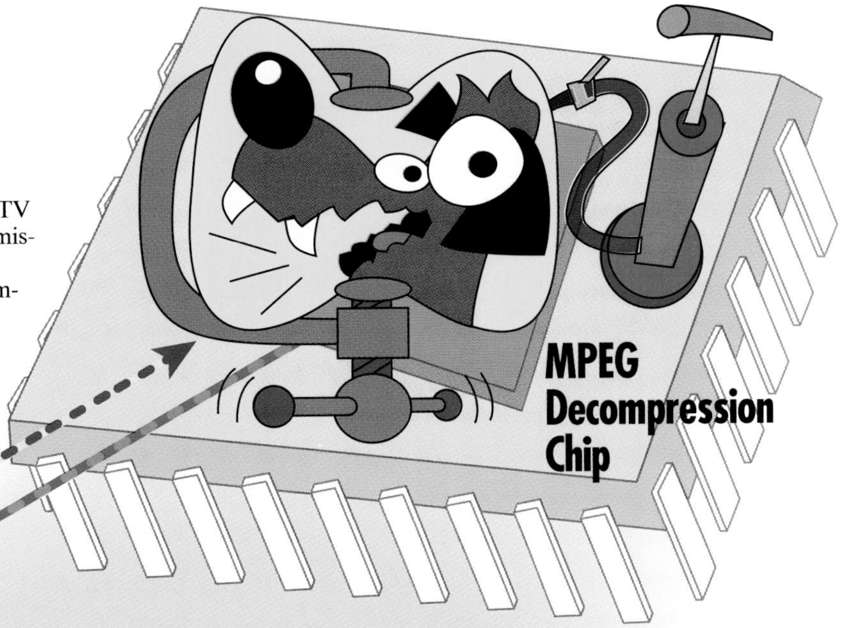

One of the critical components of an HDTV set is the compression chip. HDTV transmissions are compressed using the MPEG (Motion Picture Experts Group) data compression standard. A dedicated MPEG decompression chip handles the chore of expanding the compressed data back to its original form.

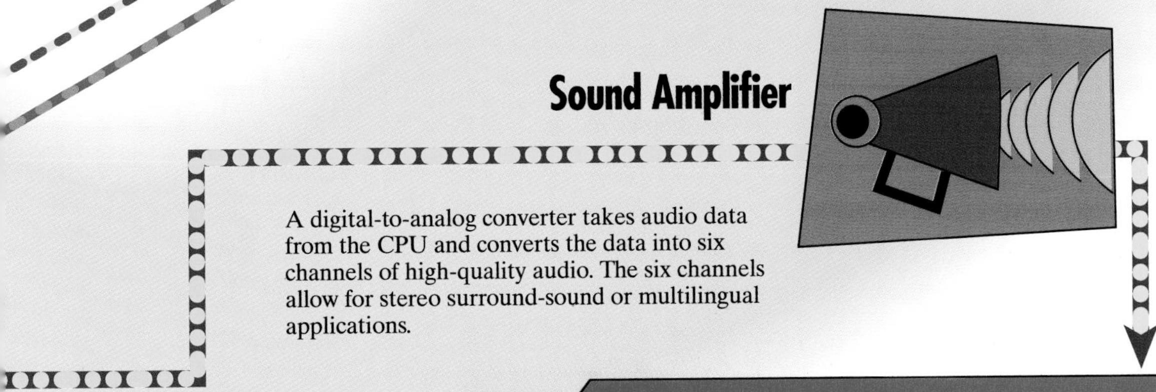

A digital-to-analog converter takes audio data from the CPU and converts the data into six channels of high-quality audio. The six channels allow for stereo surround-sound or multilingual applications.

The CPU sends the expanded picture data to a video display circuit, much like the video display found in PCs. The video display circuit takes the picture data and compresses it into a displayable image.

HDTV versus NTSC

Putting aside the digital versus analog issues, the biggest difference between HDTV and NTSC is on the screen. Our current NTSC system produces 485 active lines, while HDTV provides more than twice as many. If this were the only difference between the two systems, HDTV would still provide a noticeably clearer picture.

Another striking difference between the two systems is the number of picture elements, or pixels, per line. Being analog, the NTSC system doesn't produce any fixed number of pixels, but the horizontal resolution of NTSC is roughly equivalent to 1,000 pixels; HDTV produces 1,920.

TV set manufacturers measure picture tubes diagonally. A 30-inch NTSC picture tube produces an image 18 inches high and about 23½ inches across. An HDTV tube of similar height produces a picture 32 inches across. The wider screen is better suited to wide-screen movies.

NTSC pictures are sent at 30 frames per second. HDTV pictures can be sent at 24, 30, or 60 frames per second. The higher rate allows a smoother, sharper picture, and provides sharper slow-motion and still-frame pictures.

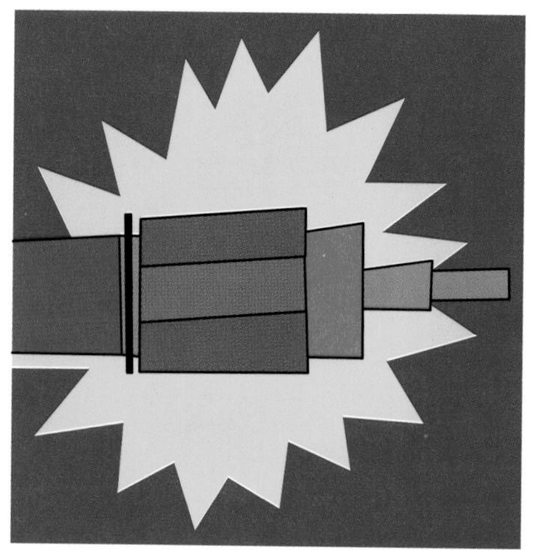

New Wave Networking

THE DIGITAL HIGHWAY will blend the old and the new. While many people will use older infrastructure equipment such as dial-up modems, Ethernet networks, and standard television sets to access the digital highway, some newer technologies will provide faster and more flexible connections.

Chapter 15 discussed packet switching and circuit switching. Today's packet-switched systems run into problems in the process of carrying sound and images that must arrive in synch. As packets make their way through the switch, they delay other packets. These delays can cause irregular gaps of several milliseconds between the arrival of packets in a stream. If you have a time-sensitive application, like videoconferencing, unsynchronized packets make lips move in speech without sound, and images jerk on the screen. An architecture called asynchronous transfer mode (ATM) bridges the gap between the traditional technologies of packet switching and circuit switching.

The ATM packet, called a *cell,* totals 53 bytes, of which only 48 bytes is user data. Because of this small, fixed cell size, if one or two cells are delayed or delivered out of sequence during the transmission of real-time audio or video, the listeners or viewers generally can't perceive the difference caused by the small loss of data. Compare this to the X.25 and frame relay packets discussed in Chapter 15. They generally allow the user data, the useful cargo in the packet, to occupy as many as 4,096 bytes, with the default as 128 bytes.

ATM is related to two switched-circuit services called switched multimegabit data service (SMDS) and broadband ISDN (BISDN). Both these switched-circuit services carry ATM cells. SMDS is a LAN-bridging service marketed by local telephone companies. Broadband ISDN is digital telephone service piped over fiber-optic cable at 155 Mbps. ATM was first described within the BISDN architecture and BISDN serves as a carrier for ATM packets.

Another interesting evolution in technology falls under the overly broad heading of wireless connectivity. This term includes systems that have a variety of ranges and capabilities. For example, conference-room systems link laptops together and into a LAN over a distance of a dozen yards. Campus-wide systems can link devices across a square mile or so. Cellular telephone systems have city-wide and country-wide ranges while proposed satellite schemes offer economical global coverage. In some geographical areas, wireless services will compete successfully with, and even displace, cables in the ground as digital highway connections.

New Wave Networking

Information everywhere! New wave networkers get information out of the air and through the ground. It isn't a question of which information channel will win, but rather of which source meets the need of a particular time and place.

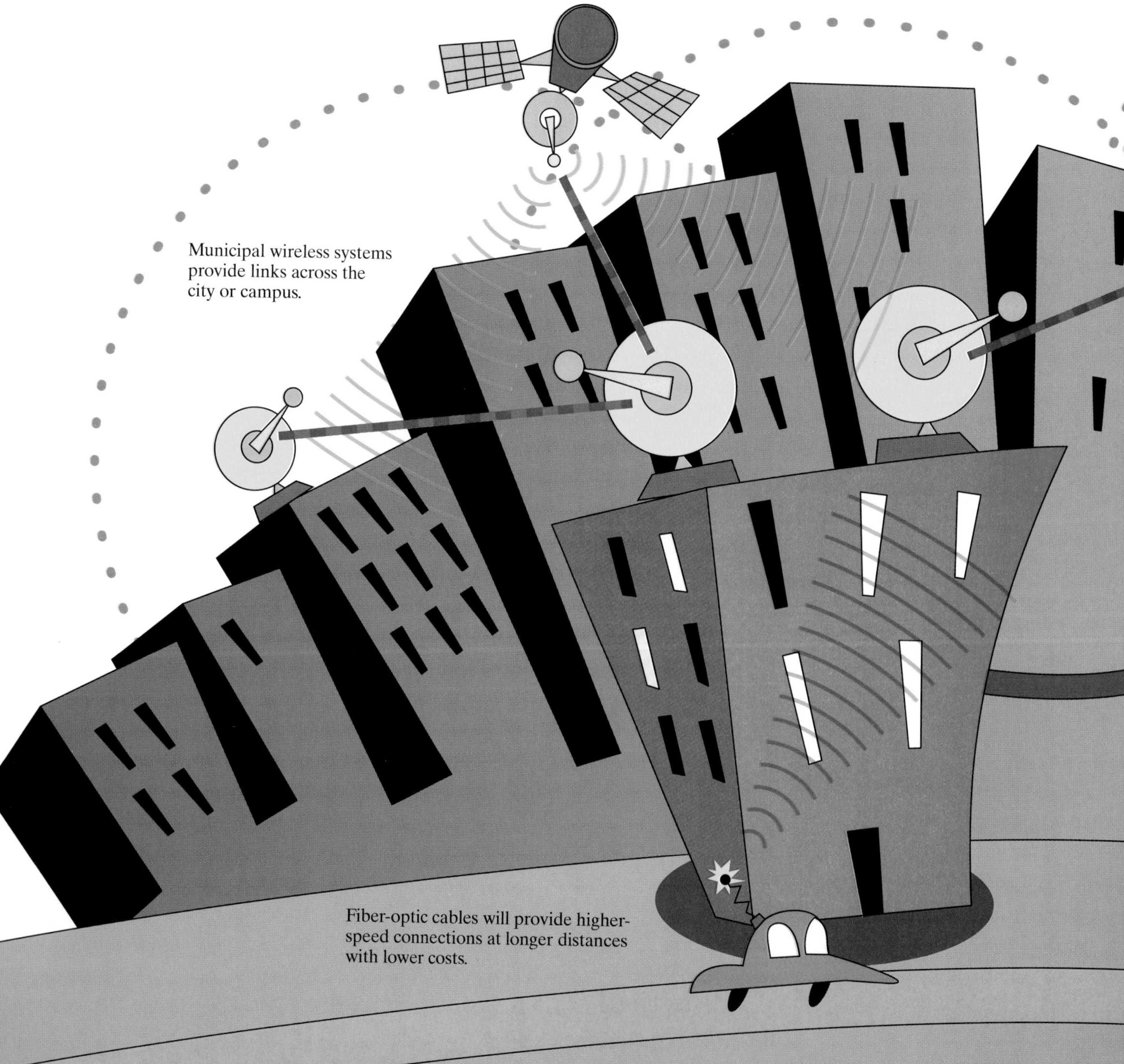

Plans from several companies call for strings of satellites in low orbit to provide worldwide data communications capabilities.

Cellular wireless systems link hand-held and laptop computers to the digital highway.

Inside the Asynchronous Transfer Mode (ATM) Switch

The ATM switch handles input from a variety of sources, changes the input into digital data, and arranges the data into small equal-size packets called cells. If one or two cells are delayed during transmission, they won't have a visible effect on the presentation of audio or video programs.

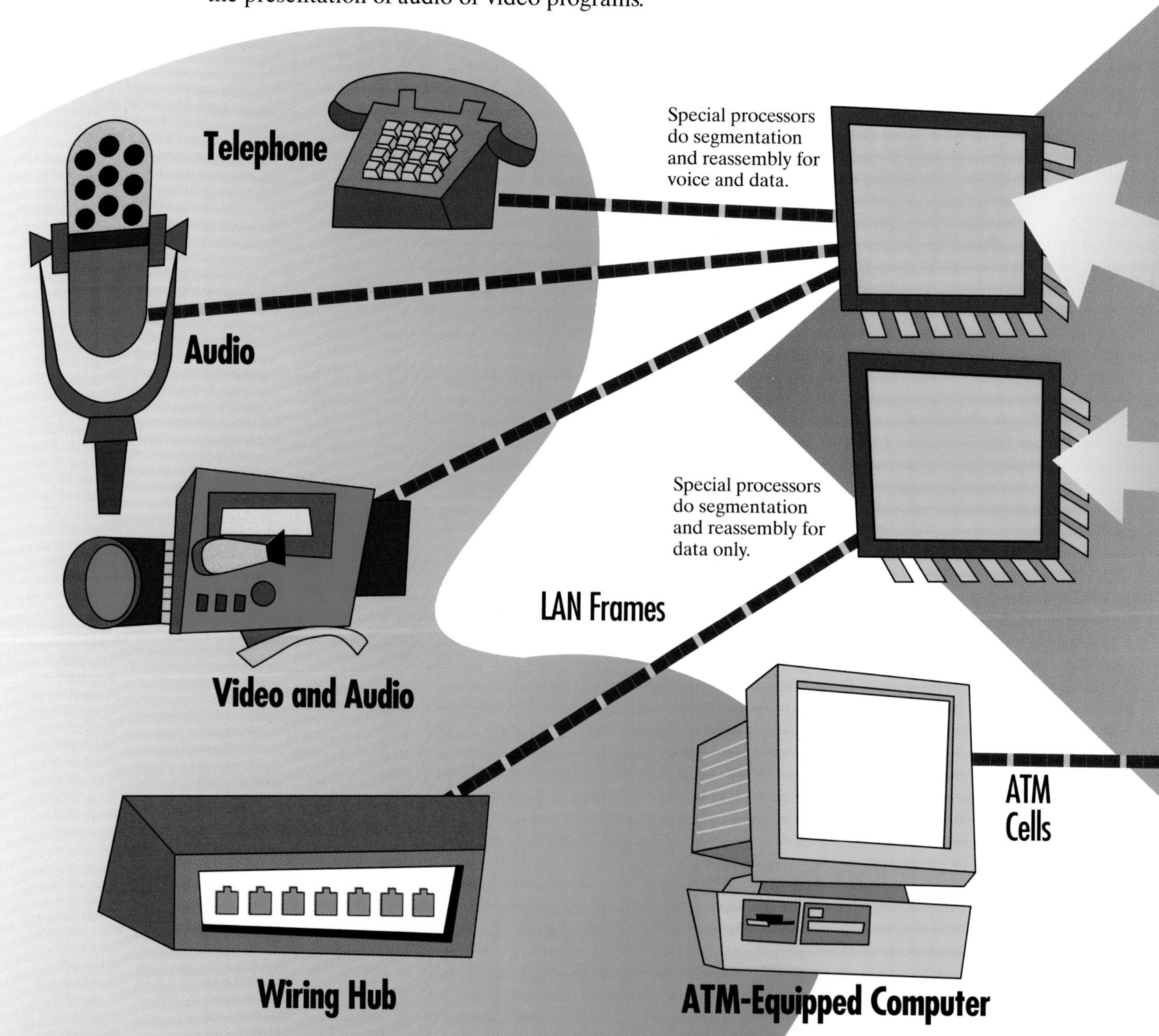

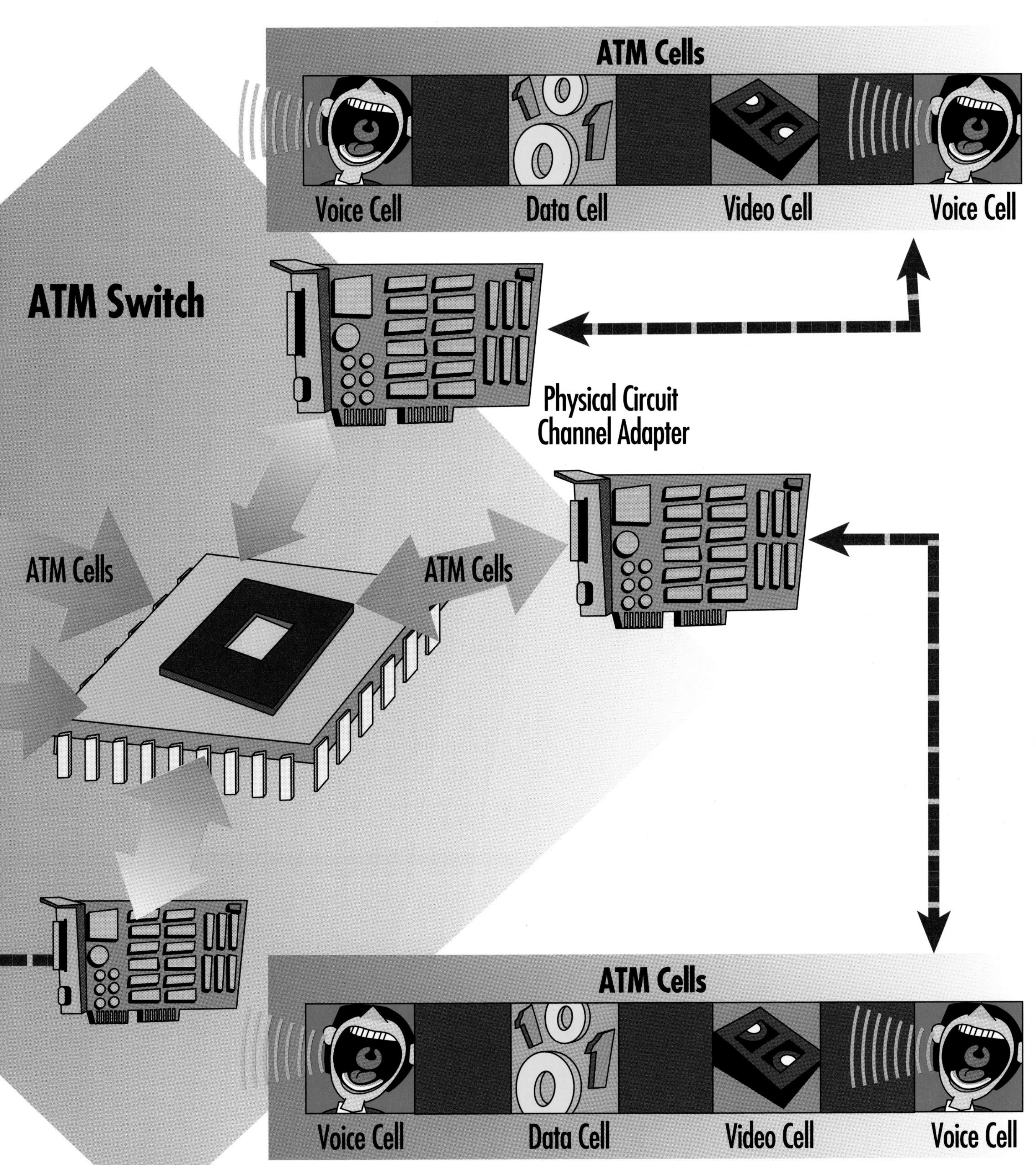
ATM Cells
Voice Cell
Data Cell
Video Cell
Voice Cell
ATM Switch
Physical Circuit
Channel Adapter
ATM Cells
ATM Cells
ATM Cells
Voice Cell
Data Cell
Video Cell
Voice Cell

A

B

C

Imagination. Innovation. Insight.

The How It Works Series from Ziff-Davis Press

"... a magnificently seamless integration of text and graphics ..."

Larry Blasko, The Associated Press, reviewing *PC/Computing How Computers Work*

No other books bring computer technology to life like the *How It Works* series from Ziff-Davis Press. Lavish, full-color illustrations and lucid text from some of the world's top computer commentators make *How It Works* books an exciting way to explore the inner workings of PC technology.

ISBN: 094-7 Price: $22.95

PC/Computing How Computers Work

A worldwide blockbuster that hit the general trade bestseller lists! *PC/Computing* magazine executive editor Ron White dismantles the PC and reveals what really makes it tick.

ISBN: 129-3 Price: $24.95

How Networks Work

Two of the most respected names in connectivity showcase the PC network, illustrating and explaining how each component does its magic and how they all fit together.

How Macs Work

A fun and fascinating voyage to the heart of the Macintosh! Two noted *MacUser* contributors cover the spectrum of Macintosh operations from startup to shutdown.

ISBN: 146-3 Price: $24.95

How Software Works

This dazzlingly illustrated volume from Ron White peeks inside the PC to show in full-color how software breathes life into the PC. Covers Windows™ and all major software categories.

ISBN: 133-1 Price: $24.95

How to Use Your Computer

Conquer computerphobia and see how this intricate machine truly makes life easier. Dozens of full-color graphics showcase the components of the PC and explain how to interact with them.

ISBN: 155-2 Price: $22.95

All About Computers

This one-of-a-kind visual guide for kids features numerous full-color illustrations and photos on every page, combined with dozens of interactive projects that reinforce computer basics, making this an exciting way to learn all about the world of computers.

ISBN: 166-8 Price: $15.95

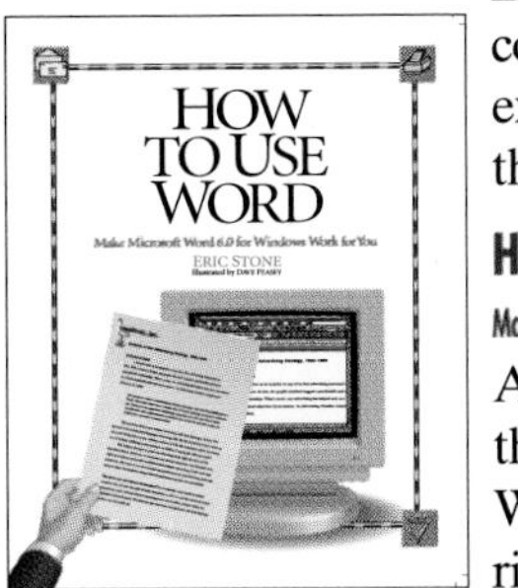

ISBN: 184-6 Price: $17.95

How To Use Word

Make Word 6.0 for Windows Work for You!

A uniquely visual approach puts the basics of Microsoft's latest Windows-based word processor right before the reader's eyes. Colorful examples invite them to begin producing a variety of documents, quickly and easily. Truly innovative!

How To Use Excel

Make Excel 5.0 for Windows Work for You!

Covering the latest version of Excel, this visually impressive resource guides beginners to spreadsheet fluency through a full-color graphical approach that makes powerful techniques seem plain as day. Hands-on "Try It" sections give new users a chance to sharpen newfound skills.

ISBN: 185-4 Price: $17.95

Available at all fine bookstores or by calling 1-800-688-0448, ext. 100. Call for more information on the Instructor's Supplement, including transparencies for each book in the *How It Works* Series.

Fight Instant Obsolescence

Is your computer wilting under the memory demands of Windows? These days some PCs are practically obsolete by the time you get them home! The good news is best-selling author Dale Lewallen is here to show you how to turn that aging workhorse of a PC into a blazingly fast racehorse, eager to run today's high-performance software and peripherals. In *This Old PC* you'll learn step-by-step how easy and inexpensive it can be to upgrade your system for years of added performance. Plus you'll get a disk that contains programs to tell you what's inside your computer and utilities for upgrading your system through software. To ensure you have all the necessary facts to make an upgrade purchase, "How to Buy" information sheets that summarize features to look for and questions to ask at the store are also included.

ZIFF-DAVIS ZD PRESS

Cut Here

Cut Here

Ziff-Davis Press Survey of Readers

Please help us in our effort to produce the best books on personal computing.
For your assistance, we would be pleased to send you a FREE catalog
featuring the complete line of Ziff-Davis Press books.

1. How did you first learn about this book?

- Recommended by a friend . . . . ☐ -1 (5)
- Recommended by store personnel . . . . ☐ -2
- Saw in Ziff-Davis Press catalog . . . . ☐ -3
- Received advertisement in the mail . . . . ☐ -4
- Saw the book on bookshelf at store . . . . ☐ -5
- Read book review in: ____________ ☐ -6
- Saw an advertisement in: ____________ ☐ -7
- Other (Please specify): ____________ ☐ -8

2. Which THREE of the following factors most influenced your decision to purchase this book? (Please check up to THREE.)

- Front or back cover information on book . . . ☐ -1 (6)
- Logo of magazine affiliated with book . . . . . . ☐ -2
- Special approach to the content . . . . ☐ -3
- Completeness of content . . . . ☐ -4
- Author's reputation. ☐ -5
- Publisher's reputation . . . . ☐ -6
- Book cover design or layout . . . . ☐ -7
- Index or table of contents of book . . . . ☐ -8
- Price of book . . . . ☐ -9
- Special effects, graphics, illustrations . . . . . . ☐ -0
- Other (Please specify): ____________ ☐ -x

3. How many computer books have you purchased in the last six months? _____ (7-10)

4. On a scale of 1 to 5, where 5 is excellent, 4 is above average, 3 is average, 2 is below average, and 1 is poor, please rate each of the following aspects of this book below. (Please circle your answer.)

Depth/completeness of coverage	5	4	3	2	1	(11)
Organization of material	5	4	3	2	1	(12)
Ease of finding topic	5	4	3	2	1	(13)
Special features/time saving tips	5	4	3	2	1	(14)
Appropriate level of writing	5	4	3	2	1	(15)
Usefulness of table of contents	5	4	3	2	1	(16)
Usefulness of index	5	4	3	2	1	(17)
Usefulness of accompanying disk	5	4	3	2	1	(18)
Usefulness of illustrations/graphics	5	4	3	2	1	(19)
Cover design and attractiveness	5	4	3	2	1	(20)
Overall design and layout of book	5	4	3	2	1	(21)
Overall satisfaction with book	5	4	3	2	1	(22)

5. Which of the following computer publications do you read regularly; that is, 3 out of 4 issues?

- Byte . . . . ☐ -1 (23)
- Computer Shopper . . . . ☐ -2
- Corporate Computing . . . . ☐ -3
- Dr. Dobb's Journal . . . . ☐ -4
- LAN Magazine . . . . ☐ -5
- MacWEEK . . . . ☐ -6
- MacUser . . . . ☐ -7
- PC Computing . . . . ☐ -8
- PC Magazine . . . . ☐ -9
- PC WEEK . . . . ☐ -0
- Windows Sources . . . . ☐ -x
- Other (Please specify): ____________ ☐ -y

Please turn page.

Cut Here

Cut Here

PLEASE TAPE HERE ONLY—DO NOT STAPLE

6. What is your level of experience with personal computers? With the subject of this book?

	With PCs		With subject of book	
Beginner	☐	-1 (24)	☐	-1 (25)
Intermediate	☐	-2	☐	-2
Advanced	☐	-3	☐	-3

7. Which of the following best describes your job title?

Officer (CEO/President/VP/owner)	☐	-1 (26)
Director/head	☐	-2
Manager/supervisor	☐	-3
Administration/staff	☐	-4
Teacher/educator/trainer	☐	-5
Lawyer/doctor/medical professional	☐	-6
Engineer/technician	☐	-7
Consultant	☐	-8
Not employed/student/retired	☐	-9
Other (Please specify): ________________	☐	-0

8. What is your age?

Under 20	☐	-1 (27)
21-29	☐	-2
30-39	☐	-3
40-49	☐	-4
50-59	☐	-5
60 or over	☐	-6

9. Are you:

Male	☐	-1 (28)
Female	☐	-2

Thank you for your assistance with this important information! Please write your address below to receive our free catalog.

Name: ______________________________

Address: ______________________________

City/State/Zip: ______________________________

Fold here to mail.

1269-07-08

NO POSTAGE NECESSARY IF MAILED IN THE UNITED STATES

BUSINESS REPLY MAIL

FIRST CLASS MAIL PERMIT NO. 1612 OAKLAND, CA

POSTAGE WILL BE PAID BY ADDRESSEE

Ziff-Davis Press
5903 Christie Avenue
Emeryville, CA 94608-1925
Attn: Marketing